GUIDED *by* GRACE

GUIDED BY GRACE

Follow the Breadcrumbs to Your Life's True Purpose

Jennifer Mentesana

©2025. All Rights Reserved. No portion of this book may be reproduced, stored in a retrieval system, or transmitted in any form or by any means—electronic, mechanical, photocopy, recording, scanning, or other—except for brief quotations in critical reviews or articles without the prior permission of the author.

Published by Game Changer Publishing

Paperback ISBN: 978-1-969372-32-2

Hardcover ISBN: 978-1-969372-33-9

Digital ISBN: 978-1-969372-34-6

www.GameChangerPublishing.com

To My Boys, Nicolas and Andrew—
*You are my inspiration. You are the next generation of men
with an opportunity to make a real impact on the world.
Always stay authentically you. Thank you for your patience
and for allowing me to share my "poetic" wisdom.*

To Olivia—
*This book is for you, and for every young woman navigating the path of life
through love, career, and purpose. May you always choose to follow
the breadcrumbs that lead to your true calling.*

To John—
*Thank you for your patience while I wrote this book, especially for
the extra school drop-offs, pickups, grocery trips, and evening meals
while I finished. You are the love of my life, my soulmate,
my business partner, and my best friend. I am so grateful
I followed the breadcrumb that led me to you.*

Read This First

Just to say thanks for buying and reading my book, I would love to offer you a complimentary digital journal that goes along with my book!

Scan the QR Code Here:

GUIDED *by* GRACE

FOLLOW THE BREADCRUMBS
TO YOUR LIFE'S TRUE PURPOSE

JENNIFER
MENTESANA

Foreword

The moment I started reading this book, I felt like I was sitting across from a soul sister—someone who truly *gets it*. Jen doesn't just talk about purpose, faith, or healing from a distance—she *lives it*, breathes it, and bravely walks through it.

Her story is raw, powerful, and beautifully relatable. She takes us on a journey that many of us have faced—when life feels like it's crumbling, and the weight of the world makes it hard to even breathe. But what makes Jen's story so impactful is that she doesn't stay in that place. She rises. She listens. She surrenders. And she teaches us how to do the same.

What struck me most was how she describes that pivotal moment—the panic attack that became a spiritual awakening. It gave me chills. I know what it feels like to hit rock bottom and still hear that gentle whisper from God telling you, *"You already know what to do."* That whisper is where the real transformation begins.

Jen writes with a mix of wisdom and warmth, grace and grit. She's the kind of woman who will hold your hand while telling you the truth— your fear doesn't come from God, and your intuition is your roadmap

Foreword

back home to yourself. Her words are a reminder that we are never alone, that we are divinely guided, and that it's never too late to rediscover the woman you were always meant to be.

If you've ever felt lost, stuck, disconnected from your purpose, or like you've silenced your voice in order to survive, this book is your invitation to rise again. Jen will remind you of your strength, your worth, and your divine assignment in this lifetime.

Let this book be your breadcrumb. Follow it. It will lead you back to truth.

With love and belief in your journey,

Amberly Lago
Top Motivational Speaker
USA Today bestselling author of *Joy Through the Journey,*
and *True Grit and Grace*
Host of *The Amberly Lago Show*

Contents

Introduction	xiii
1. Roots	1
2. Protect Your Light	7
3. Illuminated: Let Your Light Shine	25
4. Crossroads	35
5. Survival Over Soul	45
6. Beware of Bright, Shiny Objects	59
7. Healing	77
8. The Illusion	87
9. The Awakening	109
10. A New Beginning	131
11. Letting Go of Control	141
12. Full Circle	151
13. The Gift	157
14. The Only Way Around Is Through	167
15. When the Universe Speaks, Jump!	179
References	185

"All our dreams can come true, if we have the courage to pursue them."
–Walt Disney

Introduction

Many historians, theorists, spiritual leaders, and thought leaders have pondered what the true meaning of life is. Depending on your stage in life, this may mean different things to you.

At birth, your only purpose is to survive, be cared for, and loved, and to hopefully live long enough to carry out the purpose God has given you in this lifetime. Your needs are simple. At birth, you only need to get fed, bathed, and loved. You learn, grow, and experience love and joy from your parents and caregivers. Not one of us is the same, and this is as God intends it. As you grow, your needs increase, and you are no longer looking to simply survive, but to grow, thrive, and learn.

By age five, our true journey of purpose in life begins. We start school, and the world around us begins to shape us beyond our experiences with our mother, father, and those surrounding us in our home environment.

The thoughts and beliefs of those around us start to shape our experiences, and if we are fortunate, we have positive, encouraging, and inspiring voices and individuals who shape our world.

Introduction

However, for many of us, those voices can be ruled by fear, doubt, and anger. No matter how unintentionally, those voices become our beliefs, and they are deeply rooted in our psyche.

Each individual journey is unique and is intended to teach you lessons that can help you not only become the version of yourself that you want to be, but the purest form of who God intends you to be. This may be controversial to some, but if you have picked up this book, I ask you to open your mind, your heart, and most importantly, your belief system to explore what is possible. Again, if you're reading this book, you're likely already open to the idea that there is truly a higher power and purpose behind our lives.

I got the idea for this book during a major crossroads in my life. At the time, my husband and I were running a successful restaurant business, and while we managed to keep it afloat during the pandemic, the emotional and mental weight of that season was overwhelming.

Like so many others, we were navigating the uncertainty of the world shutting down, supporting two kids through Zoom school, one of whom we had just discovered had ADHD, and doing everything we could to save our livelihood.

I know I don't need to explain how difficult that time was—everyone has their own story from that chapter of history. Maybe you lost someone close or knew someone who became very ill. No matter what your experience looked like, we all faced something that changed us.

For me, the real tension wasn't just in the external chaos—it was internal. I found myself questioning a lot of what was happening. While I respected the need to protect others, something about the overarching response felt misaligned with my inner knowing. I couldn't quite put my finger on it at the time, but something didn't sit right. The deeper we got into it, the more I felt this quiet but persistent nudge: **there's more going on here than meets the eye.**

As someone who has always chosen to take action, find solutions, and help others, it was hard to feel like we were being asked to stay still and

Introduction

comply without question. But rather than stay stuck in frustration, I began to pay close attention—not just to the world, but to what was happening inside of me. I observed how fear was being used as a tool, and I started to reflect on where that fear was really coming from.

That was a turning point for me.

What I've come to understand is this: **fear doesn't come from God**. It comes either from our biology, our brain's protective mechanisms, or from the beliefs and narratives we've absorbed from others. Fear that rises from an actual threat is there to protect us. But fear that's been planted through external voices, whether from media, systems, or even well-meaning people, can cloud our ability to hear the deeper truth within us.

Your intuition, however, is different. It doesn't shout. It gently whispers. And even in the noisiest moments, it knows what's right for you. The challenge is learning to hear it through all the external noise.

So I invite you to consider: When have you made a decision out of fear, and was that fear truly protecting you, or was it a story you were told? Was it something rooted in truth, or in control? Take time to reflect. Journal. Get curious, not judgmental. These are the moments that bring clarity.

For me, once I realized that our family wasn't in immediate danger, I began to shift. I could finally breathe again. We chose to focus on what we could control—our faith, our love for one another, and how we showed up in our community.

That choice—to trust God instead of fear—opened something in me that changed everything. And that's where the journey of this book really began.

While I had been doing a lot of self-development work for many years and had received my Certified Professional Coach Certification almost fifteen years ago, God had never really played a huge part in my decisions. I believed in God, I prayed, and for many years, I went to church

Introduction

on occasion, but I never allowed God to fully come into my life. I never really put a lot of trust in Him or His impact on my life. I believed that everything was up to me, that I had to figure out the outcome of every situation on my own, and therefore, when I had no control over the outcome, it would send me spiraling into a myriad of emotions, from anger to hopelessness to complacency.

As I slowly began praying more, reconnecting with myself and my higher power, it was amazing how I was able to begin to let go and trust that God had a plan. I was able to function without being so angry and frustrated all of the time.

Once we survived the pandemic as a family and a business, and my kids finally went back to school (almost two years later), we started to come out of survival mode. It felt as if we had been through a war that had almost killed us, tried to take our hopes and dreams, but we survived. I'm sure that's how you felt as well. The pandemic took a toll on us all, but we made it, and we are still standing, further committed to our faith, beliefs, and resolve.

As the country slowly came back to normal, however, there was still this underlying ache in my gut that something wasn't right. I went further inward to begin to understand what was happening to me. I got back into reading self-development books, listening to podcasts, and taking long, soul-searching walks to connect more to my relationship with God and my intuition.

As I began to open myself up more to God and trust what was happening inside me, the course of my life, and, more importantly, the relationship and connection I now have with God, became my primary focus. But still, I had this ache in my gut that wouldn't go away, and I was trying to get to the bottom of what was coming up for me.

If you notice that you have feelings bubbling inside of you, beneath the surface of your consciousness, that is a sign you need to pay attention to and not ignore. It's your intuition telling you that you are on the wrong track or that something is not right. It could be your health, or a

Introduction

situation that you are not dealing with (often, your health is impacted because of a situation or trauma that you have not dealt with).

The longer you ignore these feelings, the louder they will become to get your attention. You can tell the difference between a positive, intuitive hit (a **breadcrumb**) and an underlying message that something is wrong. Get straight to the core or root of what it is, and if it's so deeply rooted, coming from the past or something major that you have put off dealing with, it will be harder to work through, but it is absolutely necessary that you deal with it for both your physical and mental health, as well as your relationships and sanity.

One night, not too long after the pandemic was finally behind us, I woke up out of a dead sleep with a sudden gasp. I immediately sat up, and I couldn't breathe. I started to gulp for air, and it scared me.

I looked over at my husband, snoring next to me, and realized he wasn't seeing or hearing what was happening. I started to cry. I was so scared because I had been dead asleep and was now in the middle of what I thought was a heart attack. But after a few moments, I realized I was in the middle of a full-blown panic attack. I didn't want to wake my husband because he wouldn't be able to do anything, and frankly, I didn't want to alert him to what was happening. I wasn't sure if I should get out of bed and go into the bathroom or just try to lie there and calm myself down.

As I was gasping and sobbing between gasps for breath, I finally calmed down and started to pray. I begged God to help me. It started with begging him to help me breathe, and slowly, my prayers became about my life. How had we gotten here? We had worked so hard to build this life, to raise our kids to be good people, to earn every dollar through hard work, commitment, and community.

I felt as if the world had come down on us. I was so disappointed in our society and how people treated each other. We had lost so much during the pandemic, and I didn't see how we were ever going to come back from it. I was confused about where I was in my life. I had completely

Introduction

lost my sense of purpose, and I just didn't know where I was supposed to be. I loved my kids, my husband, and our life, but everything, every day, was such a struggle and had been for years.

I was exhausted from fighting, exhausted from putting on a brave face and pretending to our friends, family, and everyone around us that everything was okay. All of the fear, anger, and anxiety from not just the past few years but from a lifetime were coming to a head all at once. I realized I had pushed down my feelings for so long that there was literally no room left inside of me for them to stay put. They had to come out.

I lay there and sobbed and prayed for hours. Finally, somewhere between awake and falling asleep, something happened. I heard something. It was a whisper. It was low and quiet, yet clear. The voice said, *You already know what to do*. As clear as day. I sat up in that moment and looked around to see if someone was there or if my husband was awake. Nothing, dead silence, and darkness.

Then, in the darkness of my bedroom, I saw scenes from my life flashing before me like clips from a movie. The first scene was of me performing on a stage as a little girl dressed in a bright pink leotard and tutu. My hair was curled, and I had a huge smile on my face!

In another scene, I was a teenage girl performing in my school play, feeling so alive and connected to myself. And then another scene of me in high school, standing up at a podium speaking about a topic I was passionate about.

I remembered in that moment who I was and who I had wanted to be. I remembered that I wanted to be a news anchor, and I went to college to study journalism. But somehow, that version of myself got pushed to the side over the years.

I had given her up, let her go, and had become this completely other person. Instead, I had lived out of fear, the expectation of success, and the need for financial security for so long that I had completely forgotten who God had designed me to be. He had wanted me to

Introduction

become something completely different than what I had become. Not that he didn't want me to have a family, be a supportive wife, and help my husband launch his dream of owning a restaurant, but I had ignored my own gifts and talents to chase success and the need for financial security. I knew in that moment that something would be different when I woke up the next day. I didn't know how or in what direction I was going, but I knew God would help me follow the path.

This book is not intended to be about spirituality or your relationship with your divine creator, but it is about finding the purpose that God created for you, and for you to share with the world.

My hope is that by reading each chapter, you will become more aware of the incidents and experiences in your own life that brought you closer to who you are meant to be, and how to see the little hints—or whispers, as I call them—that are breadcrumbs from God and the Universe nudging you down a certain path.

These breadcrumbs are intuitive hits you will get throughout your life that guide you toward the path to your unique purpose through the gifts and talents that God instilled in you from birth. When you get an intuitive hit, you will innately know because your body has a visceral reaction when you receive it. It's like everything in your body knows this message is meant for you. You can feel it in your gut, and often you will get a warm feeling all over your body. It's the same feeling when you meet someone and connect with them immediately. You just know you were destined to meet this person for a particular reason.

If you're familiar with the term "Aha moment," that is a giant **breadcrumb** or intuitive hit from God or the Universe. (I will continue to use both God and the Universe throughout the book because I do believe that both sources of power have a hand in what we do and how the world operates. Ultimately, God is in control of everything, but the energy of the Universe, and everything in it, has great power and impacts our lives a great deal, as well as God's will for us.)

Introduction

If you're open to exploring what is possible through God's will for us, I invite you to explore the ideas and concepts this book offers to help you better understand your life and your purpose so that you can truly live a meaningful life full of joy, fulfillment, love, peace, possibility, and, yes, success!

Throughout the book, I will use lessons from my own life story. These are simply my own experiences and may not be perceived in the same way by the people in my life who are presented in this book. That is exactly the point; these are my lessons and life experiences based on what God wants me to see, learn, and experience.

The people described in the book were brought into my life to teach me something, and likely learned their own lessons and had experiences completely unique to themselves. I may have been brought into their life to teach them something different—or nothing at all.

This is the most important aspect I need to point out, so you understand that the people who came into your life for a specific reason or season do not necessarily have the same experience, or their perceptions of the experience can be completely different. This process is relevant to show you only your own life lessons and God's purpose for you. This book will not help you understand anyone else's life lessons or the reason why you came into their lives. That is for them to discover.

I must also point out that I have changed the names of most people in this book who are still alive to protect their privacy and identity. This book is not intended to tell anyone else's story but my own, and I am truly grateful to all those who agreed to be a part of this book to allow me to share their stories as a part of mine.

I would also like to add that we have no control over the beliefs and actions of others. You can try to convince or persuade them to act and behave the way you want them to, and many try, out of anger, fear, or manipulation, but free will is part of being human as well as a spiritual experience. No one can make you feel or do anything unless you allow them to.

Introduction

Every single story I share or situation I experience is told for a specific purpose. The stories are meant to help you understand lessons in your own life, so you can go deeper to learn how to apply them for growth, create a closer connection to God, and live out His purpose for you.

As I will share many times throughout the book, my belief about our lessons, and that we chose them likely before we were born, is based on evidence and also theory (which I believe to be truth) from many great doctors, therapists, and spiritual leaders over a span of several decades—experts such as Andy Tomlinson, Dr. Brian Weiss, and Michael Newton, all reputable authors who have discussed this topic at length in their own books (I reference many books on this subject at the end of the book).

After reading Brian Weiss's books *Many Lives, Many Masters* and *Only Love Is Real* over three decades ago, I have come to learn a great deal and understand about past lives, souls who travel together across lifetimes, and, most importantly, the lessons we come to learn in each lifetime and how we actually choose to learn from them so we can become one with our creator. These references at the end of the book are there so you can do more research on this topic if you wish.

But again, the ultimate purpose of this book is for you to become more aware, more open, and to follow the messages and breadcrumbs that are sent to you so that you can live out your ultimate purpose in this lifetime!

Chapter 1
Roots

"I have great respect for the past. If you don't know where you've come from, you don't know where you're going."
–Maya Angelou

My first clear memory is of my family dog, an Irish setter named Whiskey (that should tell you a lot already). Whiskey was there when I was born, and I have so many warm, fond memories of playing on the floor with that gentle, kind, and loving dog.

I also have a beautiful memory of being in my mother's arms. I was maybe around two at the time, and we were looking up at the moon. My great-grandfather had recently passed away, and she explained to me that the shadows in the moon were the images of God and my grandfather, so that I could be comforted when I looked up and saw them. I believe my mother was trying to explain Heaven in a way that I could understand: my grandfather was now with God, and they were up in Heaven, where I could look at them every night in the moon.

Jennifer Mentesana

I believed that story for many years until I learned in school years later that the shapes in the moon at night are phases of the moon as it shifts. I actually preferred the story about God and my great-grandfather. Many things that we learn when we are very young become part of our story and beliefs. We believe what we are taught, and do not question it until we grow up and the world around us shapes our perspectives.

I am the first of three children to my parents, who were married in the late 1960s. My father was a real estate attorney and was from a successful Jewish family in Southern California. He was one of three siblings, all of whom attended law school. (He graduated from Stanford for undergrad, then attended UCLA for his law degree.) His parents were both immigrants from Eastern Europe during World War II; they had escaped the Nazis by boat to New York and through Ellis Island. There were high expectations of my father and his siblings to follow in their father's footsteps, who had become a renowned Superior Court Judge in California.

During his senior year at Stanford, my father was diagnosed with type 1 diabetes. It was a diagnosis that would challenge him for the rest of his life. He met my mom while in graduate school at UCLA. She was getting her undergraduate degree and ultimately studied to become a teacher. My dad was everything my mom thought she needed—handsome, smart, in law school, and from a prominent family.

My mom had a very different upbringing. Her mother, Audrey, brought her to the United States when she was just six months old on a warship from New Zealand. Audrey had only one set of clothes and sixteen dollars in her pocket.

She had married an American soldier less than a year earlier. He was stationed in Guadalcanal and came to Auckland on R&R in 1943, where they met. He was then deployed to Pearl Harbor shortly after. After the deployment, in the middle of the war, my grandmother set out for America on a warship with her six-month-old baby; it was a very dangerous time to be sailing through the South Pacific. But she was

Guided by Grace

desperate to start a new life in America with her baby, as she imagined it would be just like the movies she had seen as a girl.

When Audrey arrived at the port in San Francisco, she was sent to a military base in San Diego, and then ultimately was put on a train to St. Louis, Missouri, where her husband's family lived. She and her husband's marriage lasted only a couple of years, and it wasn't long before he found someone else and wanted a divorce.

With no other choice, my grandmother left her baby with her husband's parents and set out to get a job and create a life where she could raise a child. It took more than two years before my grandmother was able to take care of her daughter herself.

She settled in Culver City, California, and worked at the Original See's Candy Chocolate Factory. If you remember the scene from *I Love Lucy* where Lucy works on the conveyor belt of a chocolate factory, dressed in a crisp white uniform and hat, that was my grandmother. She admitted years later that she was equally as terrible on the assembly line.

My mother was raised between St. Louis with her grandparents and father in the summers, and Culver City with her mother and ultimately two stepfathers, bouncing around across the country for most of her youth. It wasn't until she was fifteen that her mother married my Grandpa Walt, and he became the stable and steady father figure she had wanted all her life.

My mom was quiet, responsible, and studious, much more so than my Grandma Audrey, and she longed to have a more stable life and future than my grandmother had. She thought she had found her path when she was accepted at UCLA and met my dad.

Their first years together were relatively simple, but even in the earliest days of my parents' relationship, there was underlying conflict. The initial conflict in their lives was that my mother was not Jewish, and for her to marry my father, my grandmother on my dad's side (her name was Norma, but we called her "Bubbie") insisted that my mother convert to Judaism.

This was a common occurrence as religion, tradition, and expectation ruled over actual faith. It was also important that my mother convert to Judaism, as traditionally the mother carries the lineage for the children—in other words, for the children to be Jewish, the mother must be Jewish.

My mother reluctantly agreed, although she never really converted her beliefs. She chose to believe that because Jesus was Jewish, she could justify it as her faith; her relationship with God was rooted in Christianity.

In the end, ironically, the rabbi that Bubbie wanted to marry my parents decided my mom was not committed enough to the faith to be married in the synagogue. They found another, less conservative rabbi to marry them at a nondenominational venue. My dad was not invested in the outcome of my mom's conversion to the religion. He didn't care one way or another; he just went along with whatever was easiest, which was usually whatever his mother wanted.

My grandparents on my dad's side were complicated. My grandfather was raised in an immigrant family in Brooklyn after they made the trek from Eastern Europe when he was just eight years old. He was, like most young immigrants at that time, determined to make a better life for himself and his family in America. My grandfather was dedicated to his studies and attended NYU for law school. He met my grandmother in Brooklyn, but they moved to Long Beach, California, to begin their lives together.

Bubbie was from a large Jewish family. She was the only girl with four older brothers. Unfortunately, I did not learn a lot about my grandmother's upbringing, as she was very tight-lipped about her childhood. The only real influence and impact she had on my life was that she had high expectations for us. She was a strong presence at holidays and

Guided by Grace

family gatherings when I was a child, always focused on the grandchildren's behavior, our manners, and how we dressed.

She was the typical matriarch. She was not the type of grandmother who was warm and comforting, but she would always greet us by pinching our cheeks and repeating the words, "Oh my *shayne punim*" (Yiddish for "pretty face") over and over again. We knew it was meant to be affectionate, but it felt anything but. To this day, my brothers and I still laugh about how hard she would pinch our cheeks.

When we were older, and my brothers, my cousins, and I were nearing the age to start driving, she tried to have us all sign a contract that we would not drink, smoke, or do drugs. If we did this, she would buy each of us a car when we turned eighteen.

My cousins agreed and signed the contract; my brothers and I did not. Since I was the oldest of my siblings, I think I started the trend of defiance. It was less about wanting to drink or smoke, and more about the fact that I didn't like that she was bribing us. I was offended, and it was more important to me to have integrity than to receive a brand-new car. Even at that age, I was extremely principled.

The dichotomy between the two different sides of my family was extreme. Grandma Audrey was always the saving grace at holiday get-togethers. She made everyone feel comfortable and always laughed at everyone's stories, engaging in conversation with my dad's parents to ease any tension or simply to keep things light.

Everyone loved my Grandma Audrey, even Norma. Audrey just knew how to give her enough attention and recognition to keep her happy. When Norma made condescending or judgmental remarks about anyone, Grandma Audrey knew how to turn them into a joke or turn the words into something positive. She was truly the basis for any real connection at large family gatherings in my home.

Jennifer Mentesana

Take a moment to think about or journal about the environment in your home as a child. What were the dynamics between your parents? What role did your grandparents play in your life growing up? Think about your neighborhood, your community, and the messages about culture, religion, or anything else that may have impacted you.

Try not to judge any of it, simply review it as if you are watching your life as an outsider looking in. Take note of any specific energy or underlying messages or themes. Again, don't judge it; simply create some awareness around what you see and be sure to jot down anything that comes up that you have not thought about previously. It's important to look at your childhood and the culture of your upbringing through a different lens. As we grow, the way we perceive our lives is created by the internal world we live in, and we often push down things that are difficult to see or deal with. We don't tend to look at our own lives with an objective perspective. Just spend a few minutes journaling about the dynamics of your family and environment, and notice what comes up.

Chapter 2
Protect Your Light

"Don't shine so that others can see you. Shine so that through you, others can see Him."
−C.S. Lewis

When you are brought into the world as a baby, you are a blank slate, oblivious to the environment you are being introduced to. From the outside, my world looked perfect. I had a seemingly safe and secure home in a very affluent community. My father was a successful attorney, and my mother had retired from teaching and was the quintessential image of the loving and beautiful, blond suburban housewife. Little did I know that the foundation on which this was built was like water and oil being held together by quicksand.

As my mother's first child, being her entire world was all I needed at the time. The early memories of playing with our dog, Whiskey, climbing on the jungle gym in my backyard, or being passed between my mom and Grandma Audrey were fond and beautiful.

At a very young age, I became intrigued by dancing, television, and movies (likely due to my Grandma Audrey's infatuation with Shirley Temple movies). My mom recently told me a story about a time when I was around three years old, when I started dancing in front of the television when the evening news came on. Apparently, my favorite program was the evening news with Kelly Lange, one of the first female evening news anchors in the country.

Little did I or anyone know at the time that this was my very first **breadcrumb** from the Universe, indicating a path to my life's purpose. Being drawn to dancing, performing, and television was not only a passion of my grandma Audrey, but also an early indication of the passion and purpose I was given at birth.

Do you recall your earliest memories or, more importantly, activities or interests that made you feel full of life? Often, if you can remember or tap into what gave you the most joy as a child, it is likely to correlate somehow to what gives you the purest joy as an adult.

> Take a moment to journal about the times in your childhood that brought you the most joy. Write down any memories, big or small, that stand out. Pay special attention to the vivid moments that filled you with happiness or left a lasting impression at an early age.

By the time I was four, my mom had enrolled me in ballet, jazz, and tap-dancing classes. I loved the outfits, getting dressed up, and especially getting my hair curled. I remember my mom putting these tiny foam rollers in my hair that would create ringlets overnight as I slept, so I could look like Shirley Temple for my performances! But my true joy was attending the ballet class, which was in a giant elevated barn that had been repurposed as a dance studio. I loved to practice with the other little dancers in front of the giant mirror that spanned the length of the barn wall. I would also practice constantly at home in front of the double-mirror closets in my parents' bedroom. While I took these lessons for a few years, after my younger brother was born and his needs became more demanding for my mom, there was less time for me to get to my classes.

By the time I was eight years old, my second brother was born, and I don't exactly remember why, but I was no longer taking dance lessons. I had become more introverted, and I know I was picking up on the energy of my parents, their marriage, and primarily my lack of connection with my father. I literally have only a few fond memories of my father as a young girl. I knew he was there when he wasn't at work, but I only recall him around me when he was playing music like John Denver, Merle Haggard, or Johnny Cash.

There was tension in my home for as long as I can remember. But it became more extreme when my middle brother became a toddler and was more challenging for my parents. My father's struggle with diabetes, but more importantly, his full-blown outbursts of anger and rage, became a constant in our home. I didn't realize it at the time, but his drinking was excessive even in those days. As a diabetic who needed insulin shots every morning, his excessive drinking was not only a coping and numbing mechanism for him, but a blatant F-you to his disease and his situation.

While he didn't complain about it verbally, he took his anger out on all of us, but primarily my mother and my middle brother. I was the witness to the verbal abuse and often was the subject of the issue, but he never laid a hand on me. He limited his anger toward me to verbal attacks.

His anger toward my middle brother, however, was a different story. They were very similar in temperament, and I truly believe my dad was trying to beat the anger out of my brother. It was a different time, and it was a lot more common for parents to physically discipline their kids. My dad had attended military school as a young boy, and this was what they did to keep him in line. He didn't have the resources or the self-awareness to realize that what he was doing to my brother was creating trauma in our household, not discipline.

The longer this went on, the quieter I became. That happy little girl who used to sing, dance, and light up when on stage started to shrink. When my parents moved me to a private school in third grade—away from the friends and familiar faces I knew—I pulled back even more. Suddenly, I was in a new environment with kids who didn't know me, and instead of jumping in with confidence, I went inward. I became shy, even though that wasn't truly who I was deep down.

I started picking up subtle messages that I didn't belong, or that what I had to say didn't really matter. At the new school, a few boys teased me regularly. Looking back, they were probably just trying to flirt in the awkward ways kids do, but when you're a young girl, it doesn't feel playful. It just feels personal. One boy called me "freckle-face," and another gave me a silly nickname that rhymed with my last name.

On their own, those things might not have been a big deal, but I was already feeling insecure, and I hadn't built the confidence to handle those moments. So I took it all in. I internalized every word. I was riding horses at the time and found solace in going to the barn to be away from home. Being at the barn or riding on the trails, I felt free from the pressure and pain I was feeling at school and home.

I did make a few friends at that school, but overall, it was a lonely time. I remember continuing to audition for roles in the summer theater program, always hoping for a big part, where my passion could be expressed, but in the end, I was usually cast as something small, something safe. That's what my energy was projecting. My most memorable (and slightly embarrassing) role was playing a tree in a summer production with two of my friends. Meanwhile, my brother always seemed to land the main parts, which only deepened the feeling that I didn't measure up. He got the spotlight. I got the background.

Guided by Grace

I didn't feel seen for who I *knew* I was inside. I started telling myself stories like: *I'm not pretty enough. I'm not talented enough. I'm not enough.* I had a vision of who I wanted to be, but every time I looked in the mirror, I couldn't see her.

I compared myself to the girls around me, especially the blond-haired, blue-eyed ones who reminded me of my mom and my brother. And I hated my freckles. I associated them with quirky, less-than-glamorous characters like Pippi Longstocking or Laura Ingalls from *Little House on the Prairie*.

Then came the *Annie* movie. I remember hearing about the auditions, probably from my Grandma Audrey, and I became obsessed with the idea of playing that role. I didn't have curly red hair, but I could *totally* wear a wig! I was sure that part was meant for me. But my mom didn't encourage me to audition (probably saving me from a world of disappointment). When the movie finally came out, I felt crushed. It was like my one big chance had passed me by. I was eleven.

Over time, those outside messages that I wasn't good enough to be the lead started to root themselves deep inside me. Eventually, I started believing that I wasn't even good enough to be the lead in my *own* life.

By the time I hit sixth grade, I barely remembered the girl who used to twirl around the house singing and dancing. I enrolled in one last summer theater performance before seventh grade, and once again, I was cast as a backup dancer. That's when I made peace with it, in the saddest way. I told myself, *This just isn't for me.*

The energy that surrounds us in life can either build us up or tear us down. The perfect joyful soul that God has created is still somewhere deep inside, but barely visible to the outside world and even to ourselves. If you don't have someone reminding you every day of who you truly are, you can lose yourself and your light completely. That is what would have happened to me if not for Grandma Audrey.

As my mother was trying to survive emotional abuse from her marriage, and doing her best to protect us, keep the peace as much as possible, and raise my youngest brother, who was still a baby at the time, I was searching for anything to hold on to.

Fortunately, I had developed some solid friendships, but most importantly, I had my Grandma Audrey. She was my savior then, and many times since. My Grandma truly saw me when I felt no one else did. She always looked at me the way I wanted to see myself, and I now know that she truly saw me through God's eyes. She had the ability to see that in others as well. I truly believe Grandma Audrey was an angel sent from God to help those who were down on their luck.

On Sundays, when we were young, she would take my middle brother and me off the hill (the nickname our community was given since it is a large hilltop community overlooking the ocean on one side and the city of Los Angeles on the other). She would drive us thirty minutes north to Venice Beach, where we would deliver shoes, clothes, and anything else the homeless people living along the boardwalk needed. Most of them knew her by name, and she greeted them as she would any other friend (or stranger) she encountered. For two "privileged" children from my hometown, this was an entirely different world.

On our first few visits, I was scared, unsure if my brother and I were safe. But I quickly learned that these people were not scary or mean, nor did they want to hurt us. They were simply people who were down on their luck and who were grateful to anyone who would show them kindness and buy them a meal. My grandmother would never give them money, but she would bring them food and give them a clean set of clothes so that they could be presentable to go find a job.

That was always her goal: to help people get back on their feet. She opened her home (after my Grandpa Walt died) many times for friends and often even strangers when they were struggling. She gave them food, a bed, and a place to come home to. Her only rule was that you had to get a job and work to get back out on your own.

She did the same for me years later when I was at a crossroads in my own life. By the end of her life, at ninety-three, my Grandma Audrey

Guided by Grace

had helped countless people reclaim their lives. My parents and others often disapproved of her opening her home to strangers, but she was unapologetic about her choices and who she chose to help or befriend.

In the early 1970s, she became close friends with a man she worked with who was gay but hadn't come out to anyone. He came out to Grandma Audrey before anyone else in his life, and she was a cherished source of support and kindness during a very challenging period in his life. That's just who she was. She never judged anyone, living her life authentically and unapologetically. She was a free spirit, incredibly funny, an amazing friend, and the most beloved role model in my life.

> Do you have someone in your life who truly saw you for who you were born to be? Someone who brought out the very best in you, who didn't care about appearances or what others thought? Think about that person and imagine yourself looking into their eyes, looking back at you. What do you see? What do *they* see? Close your eyes and try to picture yourself through their eyes. Notice the feeling that comes up when you think about them and what they see when they look at you. Now write down what you see and feel through their eyes. This is who you truly are and what has always been deep inside of you.

We must always find and lean on the cheerleaders in our lives. The ones who see us for who we truly are and never expect us to conform to their expectations. They are rare and come in all shapes and sizes. Sometimes it's a teacher, a coach, a mentor, or a grandparent, but if you're lucky, it's your mom or dad or both. The point is to find that person and nurture that relationship so you never allow your light to go out.

By the way, if your biggest cheerleader is no longer here and has passed on, they are still with you, cheering you on and guiding you every step of the way. Most times in my life, when I am going through a difficult time or situation, I think of Grandma Audrey and how she would encourage me. She always saw me for who I truly am and what I am capable of. Even now, long after she has passed, she is my greatest cheerleader.

As I entered the awkward teenage years, my parents moved me back to public school, and I was reunited with my childhood friends. But a lot had changed in those short few years, and even with the love and support of my mom and Grandma Audrey, I was still reclusive and quiet. The outgoing little girl who loved to dance and sing was, it seemed, long gone.

I loved the comfort of friends who had known me since kindergarten, but I was still impacted a great deal by the negative messages I was getting from my home life and how I had begun to view myself. Deep down, I knew I wasn't really seen for who I was. It was like there was a really thick shell or armor around my soul. With a costume on, no one could really see me. I was also beginning to see it as protection from the outside world; I didn't let anyone in, and that way, I couldn't be hurt.

One day, early on in the school year in sixth grade, I was playing intramural co-ed flag football in PE. At my previous school, the girls and boys were separated for PE, so this was the first time in a long time that I was really interacting with boys. I had never played football before, and up until that point, I had never really enjoyed sports.

I was playing the position of center, and I hiked the ball to the quarterback, a boy I'll call "Steve." Steve was cute and fun, and I hadn't known him before since he went to a different school growing up. He was really nice to me, and I felt like I knew him from the moment we met.

There was a moment in the game where I ran toward the end zone while we were playing defense and pulled the flag of the kid with the ball on the other team. Little did I know that I scored a safety on that play (I literally had no idea what I was doing), and Steve came running down the field and gave me the biggest hug. He lifted me in the air, and at that moment, I felt the most alive I had felt in many years. It felt like someone was finally seeing me for the first time.

Do you recall a time when someone, other than your parents, finally saw you and believed in you? You instantly become what that person sees. But here's what's most important about that. I wasn't seeking approval or attention; it was just the moment of connection when someone sees you for who you really are, on the inside, and not what others perceive you to be.

That connection with Steve and that moment was something I will never forget as long as I live. It was the moment that I realized that I could have an incredible emotional and even spiritual connection with someone I barely knew.

I know it seems crazy that a moment like that could make such an impact, but it did. It lit me up inside in a way I hadn't felt for as long as I could remember. It's as if our souls recognized each other. That's how it was with Steve for most of the next ten years. I need to be super clear about this. The physical attraction and what came afterward are not what I'm referring to here, but there was a definite connection that was beyond what I had ever experienced. I wouldn't call it love at first sight; it was almost more profound than that. And my not-quite-thirteen-year-old brain was not ready to comprehend what this was.

Middle school went along relatively smoothly after that. My friends, whom I had known since kindergarten, were back in my life, and I was starting to feel more confident and secure in my own skin again.

In eighth grade, I had an opportunity to try out for the junior high school musical. Fortunately, the class Chorus and Drama was a highly popular program. Something once again ignited inside me, reminding me of who I was born to be, another **breadcrumb** guiding me down my path.

The production was *Teen Genes*, a musical that I can barely remember the plot of, but that was truly a transformative experience for me at a pivotal time in my adolescence. The moment I stepped on that stage to try out, doing a scene with Steve, I became more confident, charismatic, and talented than I had felt in many years.

Something happened to me on that stage. I just don't know how to explain it other than when I was stepping into that role, I was becoming who God intended me to be. I felt nothing but exhilaration, pure expression, and freedom. It was as if my soul was finally shedding a shell that had been protecting it and hiding me from the world since I was a young girl.

The fact that I was performing with Steve allowed for the powerful connection between us to crack wide open for everyone to see. The room could feel it, and the drama teacher cheered in excitement and stopped the entire room to point out the chemistry and powerful expression between us. It was a little embarrassing, but I didn't care. I felt so alive that there was nothing holding me back from that moment.

If you've ever had a feeling like that, and a connection with someone so powerful that it feels like you're not even in your own body, you know what I'm talking about. It's pretty powerful stuff. I need to point out here that I truly believe this is a divine connection. This level of connection can be with friendships, too. It doesn't need to be a romantic relationship. It's about your soul recognizing another soul from another lifetime or realm.

With time and reflection, I've come to believe that God (or the Universe) places certain people and relationships in our lives to guide us, stretch us, or reveal something we need to see within ourselves. Looking back, I know this experience was one of those divine moments. If you are curious about this topic, I recommend that you read *Many Lives, Many Masters* by Brian Weiss. After you're done with that, read his next book, *Only Love Is Real*. It's a very powerful description of past lives and soulmates that recognize each other throughout lifetimes.

Now, aside from the incredible connection and moment between Steve and me, I knew this was a part of me that I needed to hold on to—the part of me that came alive on stage, that felt at home, and that made me feel as if I could do this all day, every day, and never get tired.

Has that ever happened to you? You feel like you're just walking around, kind of like a robot going through the motions, and then you step into a part of yourself that comes completely alive? That is what I call a big fat **breadcrumb**! When you feel like you are in your purest form, you can do whatever it is you are doing for hours and never get tired; that's when you know you've found your path. Listen to that with every strength of your being. That is your breadcrumb, your message from God, telling you that you are on the right path. Follow it! And whatever you do, don't ignore it!

As we journey through life, there are moments that remind us of the importance of letting our true self shine. Your gifts, your light, and your essence are uniquely yours, and they are meant to illuminate not just your path but also the lives of those around you. Never let negativity or the insecurities of others dim your brilliance.

Find people who lift you up, who see your potential, and encourage you to soar. These are your allies, lean into their love and support. Guard your light fiercely because it is one of your greatest gifts, a beacon that, alongside God's guidance, will help you navigate.

For the next few years, I could literally feel the shell of my previous exterior fall away. I became more confident and social, and I felt like I finally belonged. Boys started to notice me, and the image of that once quiet and awkward girl began to fade. I relished my newfound identity and rarely looked back to remember the phase of my life that had been so dim.

At home, the environment had not improved. In fact, as my brother became a teenager, louder and stronger, the arguments with my father and verbal abuse became more volatile. I combated this energy by escaping to friends' homes or sitting on the phone in my room for hours and blaring the stereo so I could drown out the yelling.

Jennifer Mentesana

I often look back and feel guilty for not being available to my mom during that time. She was stuck in the middle, trying to raise my youngest brother, and so beaten down from verbal abuse that she had become a shell of a woman herself, trying to function the best she could for our family.

The handful of times that my dad and I would get into it, I would scream back (thanks to my newfound confidence) and run into my room or out the front door, slamming it behind me. My mom was not so fortunate; she wasn't able to just walk out and escape.

The older I got, the more defiant I became, and I was less willing to put up with my father's behavior. As time went on, my arguments with my father got more frequent. I honestly think, to some degree, he enjoyed the banter and that someone was pushing back and challenging him. Much like dealing with a bully, it was as if he respected me more when I responded with a witty comeback or quick stinging comment.

In one incident, I clearly remember him coming at me, red-faced and full of rage, in the middle of an argument. I stood my ground and yelled, "What are you going to do, spank me like you do my brother?" That comment stopped him in his tracks. I don't know where that courage came from, but as I grew, the confidence and strength inside of me did too.

The sad thing was, other than defending myself with my father, I rarely used that confidence or strength for activities or opportunities to grow my gifts. I was so focused on the social aspect of my life by that point that I rarely participated in anything that would allow me to experience true joy from within or in expressing my gifts.

Everything I sought out was from external sources. It was so ironic because the one thing that gave me the most confidence, stepping into that pure version of myself on stage, was now something that I avoided. I stopped performing in the traditional sense because I wanted to fit in.

I chose not to follow my passion for performing because the group of friends I had cultivated in middle school was part of the "cool crowd," and I feared rejection if I continued performing. The opportunity to perform in middle school was amazing, but as I entered high school, this was no longer considered "cool."

That breadcrumb I had received from standing up on that stage performing was again being pushed down, this time for fear of rejection and judgment. This is common for teenagers, and I'm not suggesting that I should have known better, but for the sake of pointing out that not ignoring a breadcrumb (in spite of what others may think) is one of the most important lessons you can learn in life. Worrying about what others think about who you are authentically and allowing the opinions of others to change the course of your life only holds you back from your true purpose and happiness.

All I cared about at that time was spending time with my friends and getting approval from my peers to fill me up. Whether that was from my friends or a boyfriend, it literally became my entire focus. I quit dancing, riding horses, and doing anything that I loved.

I spent less time with my beloved Grandma Audrey during these years (probably instinctively knowing that she would not approve of my behavior). On one occasion, my family was away at our vacation home (which was nothing fancy, a small farmhouse in the middle of the upper highlands of Ojai, California). I had invited a few friends to come with us, and we all snuck out of the bunkroom one night to visit some teenage boys who lived a few properties over.

When my dad found out, he was so furious and literally screamed at all of us for what seemed like an hour. Granted, we deserved to get in trouble, but I was so triggered by his anger and completely mortified!

My grandma was at the house with us that weekend, and she took me aside the next morning and firmly expressed her disappointment. She agreed that my dad should not have handled it that intensely, but the look of disappointment on her face was enough to make me break down into tears. She always had a way of getting through to me in a way that I could understand.

Jennifer Mentesana

If we do not feel love as a child, we will look to the external world for approval, acceptance, and love. If we do not receive love and approval from our parents, we do not have the confidence within us to feel self-love.

> Take some time here to journal about your relationship with your parents or caregivers as you grew up. Did you feel supported, loved, and encouraged as a child? Or were you criticized or diminished when you were expressing yourself? It's important to understand how communication with our parents impacted us. There are no right or wrong perceptions here. This is simply to help you understand how your earliest teachers shaped your perceptions of yourself and the world around you.

Our teenage years are so complicated. We are thrown between a world of adolescence and adulthood, without the tools to manage all that is coming at us at once. If you were fortunate enough to be raised in a household with a parent or parents who had firm but loving discipline, you were much better off than someone like me, who had no respect for my father because of his behavior and treatment of my mother and brother.

I no longer cared what he thought or how he treated me. If he grounded me, I just snuck out. My bedroom window became Grand Central Station on the weekends.

Fortunately, or unfortunately, depending on how you look at it, my bedroom was across the house from my parents', so they couldn't even hear my stereo at night, much less me sneaking out the window. I got pretty good at tucking clothes in my bed to make the shape of a body, and even stuffed a teddy bear at the top to make it look like my head with brown hair peering out from the blankets, just in case they came in and checked on me. I was never promiscuous, but became extremely mischievous, sneaking out to go teepeeing with friends, or sitting in my boyfriend's car watching the stars and listening to music all night long.

You could easily assume that I was a bad or troubled kid, but if you dug deeper, you would find a young girl desperate to feel loved and cared for. Teenagers, especially girls who do not feel love from their father, seek to find love, acceptance, and connection in other people and men (boys, in my case).

I thank God that my mother instilled a sense of values in me and respect for my body, or I could have made some horrible decisions seeking the approval of men. But sex was not something I was interested in at all at that time. I did have a strong desire to save myself for the right person. That time for me was all about feeling loved and being seen, since I did not feel that at home.

It's important to point out that my mom was very loving, and I felt loved by her, but my father's anger and behavior were so volatile that he sucked out any positive energy from our home. Between my father's anger, my brother's defiance, and my youngest brother's basic needs (he was still a young child at the time), my mom had little energy for me and almost none for herself.

I should add that during this time, my parents' relationship was primarily contractual. My dad was the provider, my mom the caregiver. My father worked fifty-plus hours a week at a law firm in downtown Los Angeles for most of his adult life. Each morning he woke up at 6 a.m., took his shot of insulin, and was out the door by 7.

He didn't return home until around 6:30 p.m., grumpy and often red-faced from the long commute and traffic. He walked through the door each evening in his suit and tie and immediately headed to the big oak bar situated between the kitchen and the family room. He poured himself a stiff bourbon on the rocks, loosened his tie, and began to open the mail. He did this every night of my life for eighteen years. He had at least two drinks before he would even open his mouth to speak to anyone.

Jennifer Mentesana

Afterward, we all sat down at the table for dinner (he then switched to a bottle of beer, usually Heineken; that green glass bottle is etched in my memory forever), and eventually he and my brother would get into some kind of argument, and the meal would be ruined before any of us had finished. (My mom comments to this day how she's shocked that none of us have an eating disorder.) The rest of the evening, I retreated to my bedroom to finish my homework or talk on the phone, often listening to my brother and dad continue to argue for the remainder of the night.

This was the basic environment of my home from my adolescence until I left for college. The messages I was getting in my home were that I didn't matter, what I had to say wasn't important, and keeping the peace was my primary role.

I can't say that I have many positive memories of my father when I was a child, except when we were away on vacation and he was riding horses, listening to John Denver, or, of course, if he had a drink in his hand. That was the thing that was so unpredictable. Alcoholism is such a strange disease. It truly affects people so differently. Some can handle their alcohol; they are able to be jovial and social, dance, and celebrate. Other people may get sadder or depressed, others angry and violent, and still others, more relaxed.

There is a lot of research about the likelihood of genetics in alcoholism, and whether or not you could be predisposed to the disease. Some scientists have found that there is a fifty percent chance of being predisposed to alcoholism if your family has a history of misuse. Even more interesting is the fact that personalities, environment, and mental health also play a huge role. The release of dopamine and endorphins through alcohol makes sense in explaining why it is so incredibly addictive.

Because my father had so many physical as well as mental health issues, alcohol was a much-appreciated reprieve not just for him, but for all of us. When he drank, he was calmer, more jovial, and less likely to go into a fit of rage. It was when he wasn't drinking that we feared him the most. My mom told me at one point that she only relaxed after he had had a few drinks and was less likely to start in on her. It is clear to me now that he was self-medicating all those years.

Alcohol was his only relief from the physical and mental pain he experienced. Even though he saw a therapist for many years (as did we all at one time or another), the resources to diagnose what was going on with him were far less available at that time. Seeing things now from the rearview mirror, I think he did the best he could at that time. I think about how many more men and women currently deal with their problems, pain, and mental illness through alcoholism. It's a vicious cycle that if you don't get a handle on, it ultimately ends in catastrophe or death. More on that topic later, but time, healing, and ultimately forgiveness offer a lot of perspective.

If you know someone who is suffering from alcoholism or uses alcohol to self-medicate (maybe this is hitting a little too close to home for you), I can relate, and I'm here to tell you that you are not alone. Alcoholism is one of the most complicated issues of our existence. For many, alcohol is not a problem. They can have a drink or two or even three, and it's not a problem as long as they don't drive a car or are responsible for anyone's safety. If their alcohol use is under control and not used as a form of numbing, it is usually not an issue.

On the other hand, for others, it can completely control their lives and their ability to feel real joy. If you or someone you know is struggling, reach out to someone you trust for help. My father's alcoholism wasn't necessarily something that we feared; again, it was a reprieve for just about all of us. But what it did create was an underlying narrative in our home that my father couldn't be happy without a drink. Our family was too much; he didn't have joy in anything other than drinking, playing golf, or riding horses, and it was our job to stay out of his way and not rock the boat. I got very good at retreating to my room and talking on the phone all night so that I could get engagement from somewhere.

Jennifer Mentesana

Once again, our experiences shape our perception of the world and our part in it, creating a significant impact on our future and the choices we make. In fact, much of your life is predicated on the experiences and environment in your home or social setting growing up. The messages you are getting from the people around you begin to take hold, settling into your subconscious as part of your limiting beliefs or your stories. In fact, we all carry pieces of stories that others have written for us—assumptions, expectations, and labels that shaped how we see ourselves, even if they were never really true.

> Is there a story or belief that you have carried with you for most of your life that you can challenge? Ask yourself, *Is this belief really mine? Is it helping me grow, or is it holding me back?* Begin to notice which thoughts feel heavy, limiting, or out of alignment—chances are, they were never yours to begin with.
>
> When you start to challenge those old labels and rewrite your inner narrative, you make space for the truth of who you are to rise. Take this time to rewrite a limiting belief or story that someone created about you. What is the truth? How can you rewrite that story or belief to create a new narrative that supports who you are authentically?

Chapter 3
Illuminated: Let Your Light Shine

"There is nothing enlightened about shrinking so that other people won't feel insecure around you."
–Marianne Williamson

As I continued in high school, I got further and further away from that breadcrumb that had been nudging me to get back on stage and perform.

The friendships I had cultivated since gaining more confidence were not supportive of a "theater geek" in high school, or so I believed. Even joining the cheer squad was considered taboo to my newfound "clique," and as much as I knew I would enjoy it, I chose to turn my back on those opportunities to avoid social "suicide."

I spent most of my time hanging out with friends after school and partying on the weekends, and less time curating my love of performing, completely ignoring the realization of the gift that had brought me out of my hollow, insecure shell only a few years prior.

Jennifer Mentesana

It wasn't until my junior year in high school when I took a public speaking class as an elective that my true light reemerged.

The first time I stepped onto the podium in front of my class of approximately thirty students, I was hooked! It was as if I came alive again inside for the first time in years (the next **Breadcrumb**). I had totally forgotten that feeling and how confident I became once I opened my mouth and allowed my true self to be seen. This was the feeling I had been missing and what I had dismissed all those years ago in middle school. (I guess it was only three years earlier, but at seventeen, it felt like a lifetime!)

For the first time in a long time, I didn't care what people thought. I spoke about topics I was passionate about and even debated those that I found controversial and fascinating, not just because I believed in them, but because of how it made me feel to express myself!

Looking back, this may have come from some level of confidence I gained from speaking up to my dad when he tried to verbally beat me down with his anger. My mom often tells me that I should have become an attorney like my dad. However, I was all too aware of what that life looked like, and I had absolutely zero interest. My dad did not make that career look appealing.

I remember my public speaking instructor was the first teacher I had in a long time who saw me as smart and talented. Possibly because I was so interested and focused in her class, she appreciated the level of commitment I had.

Guided by Grace

> Think about yourself when you were back in school. Were there certain teachers who resonated with you more than others? What subjects did they teach? Did you do better in those classes than in the ones where the teachers were less engaged in your success?
>
> I believe that when you are interested in a subject, and you see your strengths and have confidence in what you are learning and doing, you will connect more with not only the teacher but your true self. Take a few moments to journal about a subject or teacher you had in school, and possibly what they saw in you, and think about what classes you excelled in in high school. Usually, they are a key indicator of who you are innately and what interests you and brings you passion. If you have some clarifying thoughts about this, take time to write them in your journal, as this could be a key indicator of some hidden gifts, talents, and interests.

In high school, the only classes I really thrived in were public speaking and the honors class I took, which was called Flex. It was a combo class with two amazing teachers who were very passionate about teaching. Mr. Hall and Ms. Kierstein were probably two of the best teachers I've ever had. If you took Flex at Miraleste High School in Palos Verdes, CA, in the 1980s, you know exactly what I'm talking about. One period was history, and the other was English/language arts, but the way they taught the classes was incredible. I loved those subjects and how the teachers piqued my curiosity for writing and creativity.

To this day, I give credit to both of them for my passion for writing and storytelling. I went on to enjoy writing in college and beyond, likely due to their amazing inspiration and, most importantly, their seeing what the students were capable of. Good teachers see the talent in their students and inspire them to nurture those talents. If you were fortunate enough to have a great teacher or two, you know what I'm referring to.

I would be remiss if I didn't highlight a particular relationship I had in high school that became an important part of my path and ultimately had a large impact on other relationships in my future, and the impact that these types of relationships can have on your life. Most of us have a first love. Someone who comes into our lives when we are young, usually in our teenage years or even in our early twenties, and who impacts us in a way that completely changes everything.

That person for me was Steve. While I dated other boys throughout high school, and those relationships were important to me, Steve and I had been off and on since I was twelve years old, and that relationship continued into my twenties.

It's important for me to highlight this particular relationship for the sake of understanding how you perceive yourself in relationships and definitely in relationships that continue to impact you over a long period of time.

My relationship with Steve was anything but stable and consistent. We were either crazy about each other and inseparable, or we were broken up, dating other people, and barely speaking. We were not the kind of couple who lasted all four years in high school or even beyond, but when we were together, I was truly happy and connected to myself and who I was. There was an energy between Steve and me that was just different for me than with anyone else. I saw myself through his eyes as the purest form of myself and my soul, and not what I saw myself as through the eyes of others. There was a side of me that Steve saw that no one else recognized, and I saw him the same way. While we were only teenagers, our connection had no boundaries of time or space, and it was as if we had known each other all our lives or even beyond that.

Steve and I would date for several months at a time, in a whirlwind of passion and connection, then get in a fight or one of us would want to date someone new. Then inevitably, we would get back together for a time, and then this vicious cycle would continue. This went on all throughout high school and beyond.

I felt like he saw something in me that was different than what anyone else had seen. Our connection went deep into my soul, and I can still to this day remember the feeling I had when we were together. It was beyond anything I have ever felt in my life.

I believe that first loves are like that. They impact you in a way that shows you what real love is supposed to feel like, so that when you find it again, you will recognize it. Whether a first love is a true soulmate or just the first time you feel real romantic love with another person, it changes you forever.

> Try to remember the feeling you had when you fell in love for the first time. Maybe it was not reciprocated, but that feeling and that connection were different from anything you have ever felt before. How did it impact you? Did you feel like you were on top of the world, as if you were the only two people on earth? Did it feel like the world stopped moving and time stood still? Was it a healthy relationship? This is super important to hone in on because your first love can often impact how you view relationships going forward in your life. You will often compare relationships to your first love, depending on what it means to you.

As we get older, our decisions on relationships are more centered around society's expectations or what we think we need based on external factors. Your decisions on the type of human being you want to be with, your values, and your goals start to come into play. Your choices become more practical. But when you fall in love for the first time, you don't have all of the societal influences and life decisions impacting your feelings. You are too young to know anything different or care, so the feeling is pure and simple.

As you get older, you may choose relationships and people for specific reasons, either because they meet a need or have shared values, versus a pure connection and potentially a true soulmate. Oftentimes, and certainly in my case, as I got older, I began to pull in people and relationships that were a direct result of my relationship with my father, or lack thereof. More on this in the coming chapters, but if you begin journaling about your dynamics in relationships, and you notice a pattern, take note. This is where the breadcrumbs come into play in relationships as well. It's complicated, as I will point out in the next few chapters, but not all relationships are divinely sent to you because they are your soulmate; they are all meant to teach you something about your path and your purpose in this lifetime.

When God (or life/the Universe, again, whatever you believe) sends you little nudges, these are breadcrumbs toward the path you are intended to follow. Do you listen or do you ignore them until another one comes, one that is a little bigger and louder, and is finally dropped right smack on your head?

Life isn't just about the choices or decisions we make that may be right or wrong, but about the ones we choose to ignore when everything inside of us tells us to listen. When you come fully alive and feel the most open and free in your body, and free from the restrictions of society and the expectations of others, notice that! That is your true spiritual form, the one that God designed just for you! It's uninhibited and capable of your soul's fullest expression! All the love, talent, gifts, and wisdom you embody are accessible without effort. It's almost as if you are hovering between reality and, dare I say... heaven. Your soul is the closest to God that it can possibly be when it is in true form, unshielded from human hindrance.

This is what I felt on that stage in middle school, opposite Steve, trying out for the school musical, and again when I was speaking at the podium in high school. We also often feel this when we experience true love. All earthly cares and protection of the ego are released, and you are just two souls connecting in a divine experience that is inexplicable to others around you.

The hard part about this is that even though you may feel like this is the person you are meant to be with forever, and that God and the Universe have created this person just for you, that isn't always the case.

Often, we have soulmates who come into our lives simply to teach us something. They are there for a season, for the purpose of showing you a path, or a lesson that you are intended to learn or experience, but that person may not be your ultimate destiny in this lifetime.

This is one of the hardest lessons to learn, because when someone is brought into your life who you believe to be your soulmate, you can't understand why they wouldn't be there forever. This is where you must trust the path God has for you. Remember when I said in the book introduction that you cannot control what happens with other people? God has a path for them, as well as for you, and it is not up to you to decide the direction of that path. I will add on to this later as we continue the topic about soulmates and people who are sent into our lives for a purpose.

> For now, simply take notice of the moments when you experience that feeling of pure joy and connection. What are you doing? What has transpired to create that feeling? Have you rekindled an old feeling that brings you back to a moment in time of pure joy and passion? Has someone seen something in you that you always knew was there but never allowed yourself to fully acknowledge?

Real self-discovery can be scary. It forces us to look at parts of ourselves that we fear others may reject or that we are afraid to admit, because if we do, it may change our lives and take us out of our comfort zones. It is hard to know this when we are young, but only through discomfort can we truly grow and become the purest sense of ourselves. Imagine what would happen if we did explore that part of ourselves that has always been there, deep down, protected by our exterior shell. What if we could allow ourselves to be fully who we are without fear of rejection or consequences? What then?

Here's the thing about breadcrumbs: If you don't listen to your inner voice, focus all of your energy and commitment to the path, trust the process, and stay resilient, there are a lot of bright and shiny objects which will distract you along the way.

There are also what I (and many people) call "energy vampires". These are people in your life who either unconsciously or consciously try to steal your energy or diminish your light. When people in your life see you grow, evolve, and even thrive beyond what they have seen you do before, it often makes them uncomfortable and can threaten their own identity. When you become the version of yourself that allows you to be seen with all your gifts and talents, it can be threatening to others and can hold up a mirror to those who are not doing the same.

Does this sound familiar? You likely have someone in your life who, no matter how much they love you, is unable to accept your growth and change. Change is hard for many, especially if you have known them for a long time. As you finally allow yourself to become the *real* version of yourself, the one God truly intended you to be, that can be challenging for them.

At a young age, this is hard to navigate. We do not have the knowledge or experience to see the reality that their fear is not about us, but about those who are not willing to see us for our true gifts and talents. It's their insecurity, or lack of effort to become who they are meant to be.

It is imperative, when you are growing and becoming who God designed you to be, to surround yourself with those who support you in your quest to become the purest, most authentic version of yourself. Find those who do not feel threatened by your growth, but support, nurture, and embrace it! For those who love and care about you, but

Guided by Grace

who aren't ready to accept you for who you are becoming, trust that they will come around with time once they realize your growth is not a threat to them. The real beauty is that you may inspire them to become the most authentic version of themselves as well!

During my final year in high school, David Toma, a retired police officer, motivational speaker, and the subject of multiple TV series, including *Toma, Barretta,* and *The Rockford Files,* came to speak at our school about drug addiction. He was the most inspirational person I had ever heard speak, and it further ignited the fire inside me to explore a future in some sort of public speaking and broadcasting field.

At that time, there was really no path for pursuing a career in motivational or public speaking, but television was a different story. This was another **breadcrumb** from the Universe, and the one that was flashing so brightly that I finally chose to follow it as I began to find my voice and purpose once again.

I researched majors in college that would give me an opportunity to further hone my skills and potentially lead to a career in that world. When I researched communications, specifically broadcasting, it all came full circle. My love and passion for performing as a young girl and then in the middle school play, speaking about topics that were important to me during high school, the impact of David Toma's speech, and the fascination I had for broadcasting, television, and entertainment were enough for me to realize I needed to study journalism and communications. Once I finally figured out my path to my higher calling, I needed to figure out where to start.

Thanks to my lack of interest in school up to that point, my options for college were limited. I did not have the grades or SAT scores to attend any notable broadcast journalism colleges or universities.

There was, however, a small, private all-women's college in Columbia, Missouri, called Stephens College, which was reputable and had some impressive alumni, including Dawn Wells (Mary Ann from *Gilligan's Island*) and Paula Zahn, a prominent journalist at the time. Plus, the

Jennifer Mentesana

University of Missouri's journalism program was the best in the country at that time, and it was in the same town!

Fortunately, being a B-/C+ student wasn't a problem for admission to Stephens. All you needed were the resources to pay the tuition and the desire to attend an all-girls' school in the middle of Missouri (this California girl had no idea what she was in for).

Fortunately, my dad was still a prominent real estate attorney at that time, and the tuition wasn't a real problem. As it turns out, a few of my high school friends, including my best friend since Kindergarten, Jen, also had Stephens as their top option, and upon graduating high school, off we all went to the middle of the heartland.

> Take a moment to journal about the path you chose after high school. Was it in line with what you wanted for yourself at that time? Did it align with who you believed you wanted to become? Or was it a path shaped by circumstances or by others?
>
> There is no judgment here. This exercise is simply an opportunity to observe your path from childhood into adulthood and to consider how aligned it was with who you were innately at that time. Were you following the breadcrumbs from the Universe, or were you simply going through the motions or following a path that others, such as your parents or society, expected of you?
>
> This is an exercise in tuning in to who you were then and reflecting on whether your path and purpose in life had begun to reveal themselves to you. Allow yourself to write freely, and take note of anything new that comes up or that you had not been aware of before.

Chapter 4
Crossroads

"There are two primary choices in life: to accept conditions as they exist or accept the responsibility for changing them."
—Denis Waitley

Once settled in at Stephens (I'm not going to lie, it took a few months, to say the least, and that first winter was brutal for a California girl), I made many new friendships and connections that further inspired my evolution toward who I was becoming.

The dorm life at the all-girls campus was the perfect segue between high school and the era of adulthood we were about to enter. I lived in Pillsbury Hall, an old brick building with original radiator heaters in each room, and a very dated bathroom shared between four students. The hot water took forever to get to temperature, and once it finally got warm enough to get in, your suitemate would come in to use the bathroom and flush, scalding you every single time!

Jennifer Mentesana

There were four floors in Pillsbury Hall, and an old, rusty, and regularly broken-down elevator that we often got stuck in on the way up to our top-floor hangout. Imagine move-in day each year with hundreds of students trying to use one sketchy elevator with a manual door you had to pull to close before it made its way up to each floor. It took five to ten minutes at a time just to make one trip! We took the stairs whenever we could, but there were days when you were standing there with bags full of groceries, waiting twenty minutes for your turn.

There was no air conditioning in the building, which was awful in the humid summers (unless you were fortunate enough to have your parents pay for a window AC unit, which I was not). But the hallways were where all the action was. Girls from all over the country hung out between classes and in the evenings, smoked cigarettes, told stories of high school, and shared their dreams about their future.

Those years in the dorm were some of the fondest memories of my life. Connecting with women from different backgrounds around the country added so much perspective to my life.

Columbia, Missouri, was a quaint, quintessential Midwestern college town in the late 1980s and early 1990s. This was not a place where many students came from outside the Midwest unless they went to Stephens; it seemed that half of the girls were from Texas. I loved the simple way of life with tree-lined streets that turned golden and red in the fall, and mostly, the Midwestern lifestyle that came along with the energy there.

The town is centered around the University of Missouri, home of the Missouri Tigers. Between Mizzou (the nickname for the University of Missouri), Stephens, and a local junior college, students (and co-eds) were everywhere! It wasn't just the weather and the architecture that were different; the people were different! These Midwesterners, to this day, are some of the most down-to-earth, real people I have ever met (some of whom I am still friends with to this day). It didn't take me long to feel comfortable and connect with many of the students who were within only one hundred miles of their homes.

Guided by Grace

One of those students was a girl, Stacy, who was from the town of Columbia. She had grown up there but attended boarding school away from home for high school. She decided to attend Stephens to be closer to her family, and because her mom was an alum.

She became one of my greatest supporters from day one (emotionally, she always had my back), always cheering me on and wanting the best for me and my dreams, never threatening or judgmental. We have remained close to this day. Although we have gone through some seemingly insurmountable challenges, our connection has persevered because of the respect for our individual authenticity and support for one another's quest to be the purest version of ourselves.

I tell you this because I cannot express to you the importance of finding your cheerleaders in life. Much like Grandma Audrey, Stacy is unapologetic about who *she* is, and she and many of the friends I made at Stephens truly saw me and accepted me for who *I* was. She made it easy to be with her and live freely without expectation.

> If you come across friendships or people who truly see you and accept you as you are, keep them close. Those are rare and special relationships. Take a moment to write down the cheerleaders in your life, the ones who support you, celebrate your success, and stand by you no matter what. Surround yourself with them as often as you can, and strive to offer the same in return. Doing so will elevate both your life and your relationships.
>
> You might also choose to text or call these friends or family members to let them know how much you appreciate them. Acts of gratitude not only feel good, they also create positive energy for you and those around you and invite more supportive people into your life.

Jennifer Mentesana

As my classes and college life became the norm, life at home was unraveling. I believe that leaving home left my mom, brothers, and dad with one less person to distract them from the reality of what was happening.

By the middle of my sophomore year, when I came home for winter break, my parents were separated, though they remained living under the same roof, which was not only confusing but insane considering the many years of tension and negativity in their relationship.

The sad thing was that my dad did not see it coming. My mom told me afterward that they went out to dinner to talk, and she explained to him why she was leaving and that their marriage was over. He didn't get it at all. He expected that she would just stay with him forever, regardless of all of the verbal abuse, arguing, and negativity in their marriage.

The years of counseling had done nothing to shift my dad's perspective on his part in all of it. He had failed to look inward to understand how he had contributed to the years of damage that had been created. Until my mom pulled the trigger to file for divorce, I don't think that he ever thought she would leave (though she had been trying for almost five years).

By that time, I was twenty years old, and my middle brother was off traveling, surfing around the world, and he ultimately ended up living in Australia for two years. My youngest brother, Adam, was still at home, just entering his teenage years. It was a horrible time for him to be home alone with divorcing parents, going back and forth from my mom's to my dad's once my dad finally moved out. I could write a whole book about the impact on my youngest brother and what ensued afterward, but that is his story, and out of respect for him, I will leave it at that.

During this time, however, I began to see my dad in a different light. The once irritable, angry, and seemingly powerful man became withdrawn and sad. The first time I ever witnessed my father cry, I had just pulled up the driveway after visiting a friend when I was home from school, and I looked up at the window to my dad's office above the garage. His head was in his hands, and he was sobbing.

My heart broke. The man whom I feared and resented for most of my life did have feelings after all. I sat in my car for a long time, sobbing, not sure if I wanted to turn around and go back to my friend's house or go inside. That instinct to escape the pain I had lived with for so many years came rushing back.

But instead, I swallowed my tears, walked into the house, and went straight up to my dad's office. I walked in, sat down in the chair in front of his desk, and told him I loved him. It was the first time in a very long time I can remember saying those words to him. And it was the first time I could ever remember him saying them to me. It was as if all that pain, anger, and resentment just fell away in that moment.

Perspective and forgiveness are true gifts. It didn't mean that all of the harmful things he had said and done over the years were erased, but I saw him, for the first time, as a vulnerable man, capable of hurt as well as love.

Something changed in me after that moment. I decided that I no longer wanted to hate my father. I wanted to forgive him and start anew. As much as he didn't want the divorce from my mother, I think it gave him some level of relief to let go of all that he was holding onto, trying to be something that he wasn't really capable of being.

I'm sure that period during my parents' separation, when they were living together, was difficult for my mom. She had my youngest brother to worry about, and she tiptoed around my father.

And then there was me, coming back from college expecting life to be "normal," which it was not. It did seem as though a weight had been lifted from her. She was lighter, even smiling with a sense of calmness I hadn't seen in years.

I wasn't surprised about their divorce. Not only was it necessary for her survival, but a few years earlier, she had come to my room one night to tell me that she was leaving him. Even at that time, I understood, but it turned out she didn't find the courage until years later.

I stayed home that spring semester during my parents' separation, as the weight of it was heavy, and I wasn't doing great in school at that time. I needed to get grounded and focus again on what I wanted and what I was doing and going to school for.

I enrolled in a local community college, took classes I was interested in, exercised a lot, and spent time with friends who were still at home. It was a sobering time in my life, but I look back on it as a turning point in my perspective on adults and adulthood.

People often ask me if I was affected by my parents' divorce. I tell them not nearly as much as I was affected by their marriage. Their marriage and divorce also taught me about life and how important it is to be true to yourself and what you teach your children. Staying in an abusive marriage, whether emotional or physical, is not protecting your children. It's teaching them to accept their circumstances, no matter how wrong.

My mom stayed with my father all of those years and put up with his behavior, which enabled him to continue. She did what she thought she had to do, for the good of us kids, believing, as many people did back then, that staying together regardless of her own needs was what you did. I'm not saying that you shouldn't try with everything you have to make things work. But if one partner is willing to do the work, and the other refuses to learn and grow, what choice do you have?

This period in my life could have been a major turning point if not for one particular incident that inspired me to return to Missouri to finish my degree. While I was home, I reconnected with Steve, who was in school in San Diego. I would go down on the weekends to stay with him or friends from high school who were also in school there. I was happy to reconnect with him, and while we saw each other casually, the feeling I had when I was with him was the same as the day I met him on the flag football field in the sixth grade.

Guided by Grace

That relationship was the perfect distraction and opportunity to escape my parents' divorce. I was probably more invested in our relationship at that time than Steve was, but I didn't want to see it. He was focused on school and having fun, and while we talked about me moving down to San Diego, I'm not sure how serious he was.

I was twenty at the time and had a lot going on in my life. My world was upside down, and I think I was looking for anything to grasp onto. I applied to transfer to the University of San Diego, which is a private university in the area. Steve was at San Diego State University, so we wouldn't be in school together, but we could see each other often. This was my plan. I was all set, and by mid-spring, I had been accepted to USD and was making plans to move south and out of the toxic environment of my parents' home (which no longer felt like mine).

Spring break came along, and Steve and I made plans to meet in Palm Desert with a bunch of friends. We agreed to meet at a party that a mutual friend was hosting. I arrived at the party with my girlfriends and asked the host where Steve was (remember this is before cell phones).

The look on his face told me everything I needed to know, but what came next literally felt like a knife jabbed into my gut. He said, "Steve's in the hot tub with Cindy." (Cindy was a girl he dated in high school after we broke up the last time.) I don't know what my plan was, but I walked out of the house and slowly crossed the large grass area to a path that led to the pool and hot tub. I snuck up to the gate and saw Steve and Cindy in the hot tub together. My heart sank. It was a blatant f-you to me and to our relationship and all that we had been through together over the years. We weren't kids anymore, and he had been my closest confidante during that challenging time in my life. I just couldn't believe it. After many years of processing that incident, I now know that if I had chosen to confront Steve in that moment, to have him explain himself, that could have empowered me in a way that would have had an entirely different impact on my life and future relationships. Not standing up for myself and my self-respect left a blank slate in my heart about what to make of that situation. There was no closure, no ending, and most importantly, there was the beginning of a limiting belief about my relationships with men.

However, that moment saved me from making the biggest mistake of my life, transferring from Stephens and away from the path I had been on to pursue my purpose. I left that night without even letting him know I saw him. I went home to LA and decided to return to Stephens and go back to the life I was destined to live.

I didn't see or speak to Steve again for almost thirty years. I don't think I ever truly allowed myself to deal with the pain of that incident. I buried it, unwilling to face how much it hurt to believe that he thought so little of me that he could dismiss our relationship that easily. Although we were very young, the connection between Steve and me was very real to me, and that incident was something that scarred me for a very long time.

From that moment on, my choices about relationships in college and beyond were guarded by self-preservation. I didn't allow anyone in. I chose to keep a protective shield over my heart and not allow the possibility of feeling that pain again. I pulled in relationships that were based on exterior motives rather than true connection or love. I dated several guys in college, and one who was very special to me, but I never allowed myself to trust anyone for a long time after that.

Do you remember a time in your life when you were at a crossroads, about to make a horrible decision, and the Universe (or God) stepped in and forced you to switch gears? As painful as that moment was for me, and believe me, I replayed it over and over in my subconscious for years, processing it in my dreams, I didn't realize at the time that it was exactly what I needed to get back on track with my life and God's purpose for me.

If that moment with Steve and Cindy in the hot tub hadn't happened, I would have moved to San Diego, not really knowing if Steve wanted me there, and we would have likely broken up at some other point. The truth was, we weren't meant to be. He had another path he needed to go down, and so did I. He was brought into my life, I now know after many years of processing, to show me what true love and real connection is, and what it could feel like to be in love, but with the right person, so that when it finally happened again, I would recognize it.

After living through it and doing the inner work, I can see now that not every relationship is meant to last, but every one of them comes with a purpose. This one came into my life to awaken something in me, and as painful as it was, it taught me exactly what I needed to learn.

I was at an event not long ago where the talented author and speaker, Anniston Riekstins, was speaking about this very topic. She shared a story about an incident with someone who came into her life, who caused unbearable trauma (much more traumatic than seeing your boyfriend in a hot tub with another woman). The experience was so traumatic for her that she buried it for years, only for it to manifest itself in her body as a horrible illness.

After working through the pain, both physical and emotional, through journaling and processing what had happened to her, she was able to let go of the connection around the trauma. She was able to see the person who caused that trauma as a guardian angel, sent to her to teach her something.

She then asked us to imagine seeing that person who caused you trauma in front of you and watch as they slowly remove a mask to reveal that they are a guardian angel sent by God to teach you something and reveal an important lesson that you need to learn.

After I had journaled about that moment for a long time, I now understand that Steve was in my life for a specific reason. He was there to show me what pure, authentic love is, and how it feels to be divinely connected to someone's soul. Again, not all souls are meant to travel together for a lifetime. They are often here only for a season, so that you can learn, grow, and become closer to God and His purpose for you.

Jennifer Mentesana

Is there a romantic relationship, past or present, that left you feeling hurt, confused, or unresolved? Sometimes we try to make sense of painful experiences by creating stories in our minds about what happened or what they meant. Those stories are not always true, yet they can keep us stuck.

Take some time to journal about a relationship that had a deep emotional impact on you. What caused the pain? Was it a single moment or a series of experiences? What did you make those moments mean about yourself? Where might you be filling in the blanks with assumptions or unspoken narratives?

Now gently ask yourself, *What if the story I have been telling myself is not the full truth*? How can you begin to shift your perspective, not to dismiss the pain, but to uncover the growth, the wisdom, or even the hidden gift within it?

Chapter 5
Survival Over Soul

"At the crossroads of loss and survival, I chose the path of resilience. It wasn't the road I had dreamed of, but it was the one that made me who I am. And sometimes, the detour is where you find the strength you never knew you had."
–Jen Mentesana

Once our family home was sold that summer, my parents were living separate lives, and everything that I had once known was gone. This reinvigorated my desire to go back to school in Missouri and focus on my own path. I decided to leave behind everything I experienced during that brief period between my parents' divorce and the situation with Steve, which I now choose to see as a part of the past. I returned to Stephens to pick up where I had left off.

Once I got back and got settled, I started to thrive in school, especially in my journalism classes. I relished everything, from my time in the TV studio, to reporting around campus and the community, to hours in the edit bay bringing the stories together. I was in a sorority, having plenty of fun and social time, and finally putting the worries and issues of my family behind me.

I dated a lot, but as soon as the relationship would get more serious, I would come up with a reason to move on. I wasn't interested in getting close to anyone at that point in my life, and I really wasn't over what had happened with Steve.

My dad was more communicative after the divorce and would often write me letters (typed, of course, with his signature at the bottom, only as a true lawyer would do) expressing concerns about my spending and dining-out habits. After two years of eating cafeteria food in the commons on campus, it was really difficult not to want to go out to eat as often as possible.

Campus meals were not like they are now, where there are healthy and delicious food options. Our experience was usually meatloaf, mashed potatoes, green beans, soup, or cereal. Even as I write this, I can still smell the stench of the dining hall housed in the basement of that stuffy brick building. I didn't understand my father's issues with my spending because money had not been much of an issue in the first two years I was away.

In our junior year, four of my closest friends and I moved off campus into an apartment in downtown Columbia. It was the time of our lives. We could walk everywhere, there was plenty to eat and things to do, and a group of boys from Mizzou lived in the apartment across the hall. It was like the TV show *Friends*, but in college! We always joke that we were "friends" before *Friends* was *Friends,* since the TV show did not come out for a couple more years.

But not long after we moved downtown, I got a phone call from my father. He told me that he basically could no longer afford to pay my bills, my rent, or any credit card bills, and only part of my tuition. The divorce had wiped out most of his savings, the economy was in a downturn, and he was struggling financially to keep himself afloat, much less pay for college. His diabetes had started to catch up with him, and one of his kidneys was failing.

Everything changed after that. My identity, who I thought I was, had been wrapped up in my affluent upbringing and my perception of the world as I knew it. No longer was I the fortunate girl from Southern California who could hang with the elite crowd; I was now the poor girl whose parents divorced and cut her off. At least that's how I saw myself at the time, and how I felt others saw me.

It wasn't just the fact that I now had to pay my own bills, and I hadn't had to before, but it was the sense of insecurity and feeling alone and lost that began to creep in. There was never really any financial education in my household growing up. We had everything we needed, and it was never an issue. I was even given a brand-new Audi to drive when I turned sixteen with no expectation of paying for gas, much less a car payment. I never had a checking account or credit card bill of my own up until this point, and pretty much everyone I grew up with was in the same boat. It just wasn't even a discussion because it was the norm.

While I'm so grateful for the upbringing I had in terms of access and opportunity, I now look back on it as a huge disservice to my future adult self, who had no concept of financial responsibility, much less how to balance a checkbook. It was so easy to get a checking account back then. I remember just walking into the local bank in Columbia and showing them my Stephens College ID card and they gave me a checking account and a free phone (plug-into-the-wall kind of phone, this was way before cell phones).

I got a job waiting tables and bartending at the most popular place I could think of. I had worked off and on during high school summers at a local grocery store, checking in guests at a tennis club, and in my friend's family business, doing catering during the holidays.

It turned out that I really enjoyed working, and while waiting tables was hard work, it was fun and appealed to my social and expressive personality. I especially liked making cash tips, which were flowing on popular nights in a college town. In the early 1990s, tips were still primarily cash, and many nights I would come home with hundreds of dollars. It felt amazing!

Although the jobs I had during high school had paid minimum wage and I could make a little extra "play" money, this was the first time I ever felt independent and like I could stand on my own two feet.

While I often resented the times when my friends were doing things for our sorority or going to concerts and trips on the weekends when I had to work, I was expanding my perception of the world and, more importantly, reality.

The tough part was when I didn't work a busy shift and came home with only a few bucks, and the rent or phone bills were due. I would write a check knowing I didn't have enough money in the bank to cover it. I would pray that they didn't cash the check before I could work again and replenish my account. There were countless bounced checks, unpaid parking tickets, and more than a few times that my car was towed or there was a boot on it. It was mortifying, and I hated how I felt about myself. I had never felt this sense of shame before, and it haunted me daily.

I worked at that bar for most of my remaining years in school, and the people I worked with became like family. About a year into my employment, my boss called me into his office and told me he wanted me to be the first female bartender they had ever had. I was so honored and excited for the opportunity and believed I had truly earned this promotion.

He then asked me to show up the next day in a low-cut, tight sundress to start my first shift as a bartender. It was my first experience with any level of harassment, but at the time, there was no such term. I remember feeling deflated, like the only reason I had been given this promotion was because of my looks or sexuality.

I don't know what inspired me to do this because I needed the job so badly (maybe my experience standing up to my father, or the fact that I was at an all-women's liberal arts college), but I showed up the next day in a baggy sweatshirt, jeans, and no makeup! Fortunately, my boss was not there that day, and the head bartender who trained me was a friend of mine.

However, over the next several months, I learned quickly that the more attractive I looked, the more tips I made. While I was still offended by the initial suggestion to dress for tips, I was more interested in making money than anything else. This experience prepared me for the reality of society in the years to come.

Do you remember the first time you truly felt on your own? Like, there was no one who was going to bail you out if you needed help. For me, and I'm guessing for you, that was a turning point in life. The moment you find out just how capable you truly are is the most rewarding feeling in the world.

Every time you feel overwhelmed in life and you're not sure if you can get through to the other side of whatever you are going through, think back to the moment you conquered your first seemingly insurmountable challenge on your own. If you did it then, despite having little to no experience, you can absolutely do it now, armed with everything you've endured and learned, no matter where you are in life.

The lessons, challenges, and obstacles we encounter are the necessary speed bumps that prepare us for the next phase of life and success. You are the only one who can ever truly bail yourself out. With that comes a great deal of confidence, resilience, and grit, all of which you need in life to be successful.

Of course, you ideally have people who will be there for you for emotional support, but if you rely on others to "save" you, you will continue to perpetuate the lesson that you have been handed by God to learn, grow, and succeed in life. We are all here to learn lessons, to evolve, and to become the version of ourselves that God intends us to be. Persevering on your own and overcoming challenges and failures is the only way to do that.

Jennifer Mentesana

At the crossroads of loss and survival, I chose the path of resilience. It wasn't the road I had dreamed of, but it was the one that made me who I am. And sometimes, the detour is where you find the strength you never knew you had. While I resented my dad for cutting me off, and it took me years to get on my feet financially, repair my credit, and pay off my debt, I can say that I did it on my own, with no one else's help. Of course, we all need a little help in life when we are down on our luck, but if you can pull yourself out on your own, it will be much easier to do it again (and there is a likely chance you will have to do so more than once).

During my final year in college, and leading up to graduation, my roommates and I were trying to figure out what we were going to do when school was over. I wasn't sure if I wanted to return home to LA after college or move to a new city for a new adventure. After what I had been through when I moved home my sophomore year, I didn't want to go home to that environment, but I wasn't sure how I was going to make it out in the real world on my own. Living in a small town like Columbia, Missouri, paying rent and bills on my own wasn't too rough on a bartender's wages and tips, but living in a big city was entirely something else.

One day, in my final semester, I went to the front of my broadcast communications textbook to look at the list of jobs you could get with a communications degree. It was listed by salary, and at the bottom was an entry-level position at a local TV station as a production or news associate.

At a whopping $11,000 a year salary, I realized there was no way I could survive on my own with that job, or come close to beginning to pay off my debts (credit cards and student loans), now that my parents were no longer helping me, without having another job waiting tables or bartending, and those jobs demanded round-the-clock availability at that time.

Also, the only place I would likely be able to get a job in television right out of college was in the middle of nowhere in a town like Duluth,

Guided by Grace

Minnesota. Even with all the newfound confidence and resilience I had gained, I didn't have the courage to move to the middle of nowhere on my own.

It is also important to point out that the closer you get to your gifts, your genius, and the path that you are meant to go down, the more your fears will rear their ugly head. That need for belonging, having a sense of community, a desire to fit in, and most of all, the fear of failure will kick in full force. If you haven't done the work to remove all of those limiting beliefs about yourself, your exterior armor will emerge and take over. Survival becomes the motivation, and your fight-or-flight response kicks in.

At that time, my response was to flee from my path and my purpose, to feel safe. Money and staying close to the friends I had at the time were my only means of survival. My best friend, Jen, and our two other college roommates, Stacy and Natasha, were moving to Chicago; I figured I would go along and try to make it.

At the very top of the job list in my textbook, the highest-paying salary position was media advertising sales. I don't even remember what the salary range was that was listed, but it was *a lot* more than an entry-level news associate.

I knew in that moment I was chickening out and rejecting the vision I had for my life, but it was my best chance at survival, and the only way I would begin to pay off my debt. I had to go after the highest-paying job I could get, and fast.

I decided to join my roommates, and the four of us made the trip north from Columbia to Chicago. Keep in mind that I was the only one who needed to get a job right away to pay rent, but that didn't matter to me; I knew I could get a job waiting tables and buy some time before getting a "real job."

Looking back at that time in my life, I realize now that I could have chosen to live on my own, in a more affordable apartment, and sucked it up, making little to no money to follow my dreams. But those limiting beliefs about my ability to survive on my own, without the safety and comfort of my girlfriends or the financial support from my parents, were so powerful that they completely controlled my decision-making.

Limiting beliefs are like that. They are so powerful that they create a false reality. You believe them to be true. In my mind, I would not have survived living on my own, working in a job that would barely pay the minimum on my credit card bills and transportation to and from work, not to mention rent, groceries, and anything else.

The truth is, I was still trying to keep up. Trying to live in the reality of where I had come from, although it was no longer my reality. I was truly on my own in more ways than one, and the fact is, no matter how much money I made, nothing was going to change that.

I hope that you have never been forced to abandon your true path if you knew what it was you were meant to do deep down inside of you. However, most likely, if you're reading this, you've experienced the need for survival over the desire to live in your passion and purpose.

Whether it's due to financial concerns, other circumstances, or the influence of someone who makes you believe that pursuing your passion and purpose is unrealistic, that fear can become so powerful that it obscures the truth: *You already have everything within you to live the life you are meant to live.*

How many stories do we hear about the starving actor or actress who wanted to follow their dreams to go to Hollywood, only to have their parents or some other circumstance convince them they couldn't make it on their own, or that following their dreams was irresponsible or a pipe dream? And how few stories do we hear about the actor or actress who was literally almost on the streets when they caught their first break because they never gave up?

Now, I'm not going to tell you that you should follow every dream you have that looks like the "perfect" life you want to live. It rarely is, even if you do succeed. What I'm really saying is this: When you feel a deep, unshakable knowing that a certain path is meant for you, it's not just a

Guided by Grace

fleeting thought; it's your intuition and the voice of God speaking to your soul. It's your divine responsibility to honor that calling. The Universe leaves breadcrumbs, gentle signs, and subtle nudges meant to guide you in the direction of your purpose.

But here's the truth: Those breadcrumbs aren't a map to your dream life. They're simply the path, not the destination. They are whispers from something greater, inviting you to take the next right step. Where you go from there is up to you. But once you do choose to listen to those nudges, and you are on the path of your true purpose, you will know it because the pull is so powerful that you won't want to stop.

While I graduated with the degree and education that I set out to achieve, based on the previous breadcrumbs that had led me down that path, life's circumstances pulled me away from that calling once again. I chose to listen to my fear and those limiting beliefs instead of my purpose.

At twenty-three years old, that doesn't seem like the end of the world, considering I had plenty of time to go back and pursue my calling, but the further I got down that path, the harder it was to walk away from the money, stability, and financial security that life created for me.

Upon our arrival in Chicago, three of us found an apartment together, and I was on the hook for a portion of the rent. It was a lot for me, even divided by three. Especially considering what we were paying for rent in college. If I remember correctly, I think it was around $250 a month for rent in a fabulous penthouse apartment in Columbia, Missouri, overlooking the shops, restaurants, and bars in town.

In Chicago, we moved to a beautiful high-rise building just a few blocks from Michigan Avenue and a block west of Navy Pier. I decided to bite the bullet and agree to the rent, which was more than three times what we paid in Columbia, and thankfully, my friend Natasha was willing to share her room with me.

Within a week, I got a job waiting tables at one of the most popular

Jennifer Mentesana

Italian restaurants in the city, The Rosebud on Rush Street. If you've ever been there, you know why it's been there for over fifty years.

I'll never forget that first interview. It was with the French maître d', and I could tell right away this would be the toughest boss I would ever have if I got the job. He scared me, not just because he had a thick French accent and was impeccably dressed from head to toe, but because he never smiled. Not once.

He took me down to the cabaret bar below the main dining room for the interview. There was a piano perched on a platform between two large leather booths, and several small bistro tables that were spread out across the black and white harlequin floor. There was a large bar that extended the entire length of the room, and I couldn't help but wonder what it would look like with wall-to-wall people waiting for their table in just a few hours. The room was dark, smelled of smoke, and was incredibly intimidating, even in the middle of the afternoon.

He abruptly asked me to name five different brands of vodka before even asking me what my experience was. At this point, I had only worked in casual college bars, which doubled as cafés during the day. Luckily, I had learned a few different vodka brands between bartending in college and, of course, from the open shelves of the liquor display in my dad's bar at home.

I faked the rest as best as I could, and he moved on to the next question. He asked me to name five different pasta dishes, three Italian desserts, and two different after-dinner liqueurs. I literally don't remember what my answer was to the last question, but amazingly, I got the job on the spot.

To this day, this was one of the toughest interviews I've ever encountered (and I've had so many since then, I don't even think I could count them all). I started work the following day and was sent home with instructions to come back the next day with a tuxedo shirt, bowtie, jacket, and either pants or a skirt, and to have memorized the entire menu from front to back.

Guided by Grace

This job was tough, but it was incredible training for life. I worked probably sixty hours per week. Committing to the job meant committing to the schedule, with only one day off per week and a minimum of three doubles (in the restaurant business, that means back-to-back shifts). I came home every night around 1 a.m. with my feet throbbing. I would sit on the counter in our bathroom and soak my feet in Epsom salt in the sink just so I could get to sleep. My roommates worked in fashion retail, so their hours were completely different. I hardly ever saw them in those first six months.

Now you're probably wondering why I'm going into so much detail about this job since it was nowhere near the path to my purpose. But it was one of the most significant periods of my life for many reasons.

First off, the amount of money I made at that restaurant was insane. It took me almost ten years in a corporate job to make as much money as I did that year waiting tables. It felt really good to be able to pay off a significant amount of debt, pay my bills, and even save a little.

But more importantly, it was one of the most difficult jobs and environments I have ever worked in to this day. There is no way, today, that a restaurant, or any other business for that matter, could treat their employees with that amount of blatant disrespect, as well as work them to the bone with no time off!

Since this was in Chicago, maybe the laws differ from those in California for hourly employees, but I doubt it. Now, I don't mean to say that I'm complaining, because that experience gave me a one-way ticket to reality, grit, and adulthood. If a customer's order was wrong, it was always your fault, even if it wasn't. You didn't dare complain to the kitchen, or anyone else for that matter. You handled it, no matter what.

The bartenders were tough, too. If you ordered a drink and didn't know what was in it, they wouldn't give it to you to serve to your customers. This was real life, and I was smack in the middle of it, fresh out of college at twenty-three years old. No time to prepare. Thank goodness, two of the servers I worked with looked out for me and helped me out during those first few weeks. I don't think I would have survived if not for them.

I lasted just under a year working there, and after sleepless nights, no social life, and never seeing my roommates, I decided it was time to move on and focus on getting a day job. My last night at the Rosebud was my best. I think that, because I knew I was leaving, I didn't care about anything, and I was pushing the most expensive dishes on the menu. At one table, I sold three bottles of Opus One and six orders of surf and turf, plus appetizers and desserts.

The maître d', whom I was so afraid of and who had hardly spoken to me since I started (unless he was yelling at me), gave me a huge high-five at the end of the night! I walked away on that last shift with over $1,000 in cash tips. It was *insane*!

The grit and mental toughness I developed at that job were exactly what I needed to begin my sales career. I remembered that my old boss at the bar and grill I worked at in college (yes, the one who told me to show up with my cleavage showing to bartend) had mentioned that a woman he knew who graduated from Stephens years prior lived in Chicago and worked in the media business in some capacity.

I looked her up, and it turned out that she owned a temp agency for media executives and entry-level hires! It was truly the perfect connection for that time in my life. I had a brief interview, and because we clicked right away, and she was a Stephens Girl (that's what they called us), she got me a temporary position as a sales assistant at one of the best radio stations in Chicago. This was my first real job, and although I was still not on the path to my purpose, I was excited.

The job was amazing at first, a fun environment, great people, and I was learning a lot! I found I was pretty good at being an assistant. I really loved helping the sales reps create presentations, keeping track of the campaigns they were running, and especially going for drinks after work. These were my kind of people!

Guided by Grace

The biggest issue was, aside from the fact that I was making less than one-fourth of what I made waiting tables in one year, the radio station was over twenty miles away from my apartment, and I didn't have a car.

My dad had my brother drive my car back home from California after I graduated because he wanted to sell it, and I couldn't afford to park it in our building's garage anyway. I took two trains and a bus to get to work every day. It was brutal, especially in the winter.

The first train went all the way down to the financial district on the South Side of Chicago (The Loop, if you know, you know). Then I had to cross under a tunnel to get to the other side of the tracks to take the westbound train to the bus stop. The station was still several blocks from the train stop, so I hopped on a bus to get the rest of the way to work. Now, I'm not saying that it's not common for people to take multiple modes of transportation to get to work, but for this California girl, it was insanity.

One day, on my way to work, fate stepped in. I'm not saying this was a breadcrumb, but it did change the course of my situation. One morning, I was running late for the second train going westbound, and I was waiting on the track by myself. I was upset that I was late, and I wasn't really thinking straight. I turned to look at the clock above the tunnel stairs. Standing right there was a very scary, very unkempt homeless man. He was walking quickly toward me and came up and spat in my face!

I freaked out, ran up the steps, and hailed a cab! That was it. I decided I was done with public transportation in Chicago. Now I realize it could have been a lot worse, but I didn't wait around to see what he was going to do next.

When I got to the office, I went into my manager's office and started sobbing. I told her I didn't know what to do, because I just couldn't bring myself to take the train again and couldn't afford to take cabs to work.

Jennifer Mentesana

Fortunately, she had a solution for me. One of the on-air personalities, Terri Hemmert, lived relatively close to me and had a car. She was the midday personality at that time, so she didn't need to be at the station until the time I needed to get to work.

To this day, I'm so thankful for that woman. We had a lot of fabulous conversations on our commute to WXRT, and I learned more than I probably needed to know at the time.

To this day, Terri is one of the most beloved female rock radio personalities and a true radio icon. She now teaches at Columbia College in Chicago and is still a staple at WXRT. She was one of the first female drive-time DJs for a rock station and a true musicologist. I consider myself so fortunate to have spent that quality time with her. Our morning commute conversations only lasted a few months since I eventually found another solution for my commute, but the impact it made on my life at the time was essential.

> Try to remember a time in your life when someone you hardly knew stepped in and made a difference. Maybe you only crossed paths briefly, or maybe they were present for a longer season, but the impact they had left a lasting mark. I like to think of those people as little guardian angels, sent by God or the Universe to keep you safe, rescue you in some way, or simply show you what true kindness looks like. It is powerful to remember those individuals and appreciate their influence, even if it was only for a short while.
>
> Take a moment to journal about that person and how they touched your life. Or, if you are able, reach out to them and share how much they mean to you. Small expressions of gratitude can go a long way in brightening someone's day and your own.

Chapter 6
Beware of Bright, Shiny Objects

*"Be brave enough to turn away from shiny objects,
and toward the light that makes them shine."*
–Martha N. Beck

About a year into my career at WXRT, a new friend of mine at the station, Karen, introduced me to a guy who would become my first adult relationship and first significant relationship since my breakup with Steve a few years prior. He had worked at WXRT prior to my getting hired and had left before I started working there, but just about everyone I worked with knew him and approved of the match.

I could sense a hesitation from my boss, who was his boss at one time, but I couldn't put my finger on what it was. Out of respect for him and his family, I'm not going to use his real name, but for the sake of telling this story (because it's an important part of my journey), I'll call him "Charles."

Jennifer Mentesana

Charles was charming, fun, and a little dangerous. For some reason, I was always attracted to guys who had a little bit of edge. If they were too wholesome, I would get bored (more on this topic later). Charles and I hit it off immediately. He lived alone in a nice apartment in a high-rise in Chicago. I met him when I was twenty-four and he was twenty-seven. We were a perfect match, or so I thought. He was tall, handsome, funny, and athletic. He went to college on a baseball scholarship as a pitcher, but his major league dreams came to an end when he had a career-ending shoulder injury.

I think that was what gave him a major chip on his shoulder. He needed to prove to himself that he was going to be a success after baseball. Radio advertising sales was the perfect career for an outgoing, confident, and good-looking guy who liked to have fun.

As a young radio sales assistant, I was instantly attracted to his confidence, swagger, and, of course, his good looks. We liked a lot of the same things. Nice restaurants, nice clothes, adventure and the outdoors, and endless late nights going to bars, concerts, and sporting events. It was an incredible time in my life.

There's one incident from my time at WXRT that has stayed with me for years because it's rooted in one of life's most important lessons: listening to your intuition.

As a young woman in corporate America, you quickly learn there are uncomfortable and sometimes inappropriate dynamics in office relationships. You have to be thick-skinned, but more importantly, you must fiercely protect your integrity and values.

There was an on-air personality from another station in our building, a well-known figure in Chicago. He would often stop by my desk, asking about my interest in media and my career goals. I was flattered that someone so established took the time to talk with me. It felt like he saw potential in me.

One day, he invited me for drinks after work. That was common in the business, but something in my gut hesitated. I couldn't explain it, but the "off" feeling was there. Still, I went, afraid of seeming rude or ungrateful.

We met at a sports bar in the Gold Coast, not far from my apartment. At first, it was casual. Then, the conversation shifted. He asked about my personal life, and when I mentioned I was dating someone, he leaned in and said, "Well, what if we make an arrangement? You could be my girl on the side."

He was married. And in that moment, the air changed. My stomach dropped. I excused myself to the bathroom, heart pounding, and called Charles. I didn't want to just walk out... part of me feared what might happen at work if I offended him.

Fifteen minutes later, Charles walked in, went straight to our table, locked eyes with him, and without a word to the man, turned to me and said, "Let's go." I could have cried with relief.

I was so young—naïve enough to believe he was genuinely invested in my career. But that day taught me a hard truth: not everyone who takes an interest in you has your best interest at heart.

The lesson? Your gut will *always* tell you the truth. Trust it. Protect it. Never say "yes" to something that doesn't feel right in your body, whether it's an opportunity, a meeting, or a relationship.

Even now, when I think about that moment, I can still feel the hollow ache in my stomach. I didn't have to see him much after that since he avoided my desk completely. I think he knew I wasn't as powerless as he thought. I could have reported him, but at the time, the industry was a very different place. He was a big personality; I was just an assistant.

What I know now is this: your values, your integrity, and your intuition are your greatest safeguards. When you honor all three, you will never go wrong.

After two years as a sales assistant, I felt I was ready to pursue a sales position. Charles encouraged me to pitch a promotion to my boss. My boss at WXRT was one of my very first mentors. He was really good to me and taught me a lot, but he kept telling me to be patient, that my time would come. I knew he believed in me and wanted to give me a sales position, but he didn't have one available at the time.

I was anxious and immature, and Charles was in my ear, telling me I would wait for years to move into sales if I stayed at WXRT. No one ever left there (except him, to get paid more money), it was too good a gig. Charles convinced me to interview across town at Q101, the alternative rock station in Chicago. He knew the sales manager there and got me an interview.

When I was offered my first sales position and told my boss I was leaving WXRT, he was truly disappointed. I think he thought I would stay there forever, and I wanted to, but I was also desperate to begin my career as a sales rep and start making the kind of money I had been waiting two years to make. I wanted to buy a car and be able to afford my rent again, and not to feel like I couldn't afford to contribute to groceries and other expenses with my roommate.

By then, I had moved in with my best friend, Jen. After all the years we spent together, from elementary school to middle school, high school to college in Missouri, and now in Chicago, we became more like sisters than roommates or even best friends.

She was dating her college boyfriend (whom she is now married to and has been for twenty-five years), and we were both so busy with our jobs and relationships that we hardly ever saw each other. But there was tension even on the rare times we did spend time together because we were in such different places in our lives. I couldn't always afford to pay for much besides the rent and utilities. I would go for days without eating much at home, simply because I couldn't afford to go to the grocery store. Every dime of my money went toward rent, paying off my credit card debt, and getting to and from work in a cab when I couldn't get a ride with Terri.

Luckily, since Charles made good money, I usually ate out with him, or we would cook delicious meals at his apartment. I ate fruit or snacks

Guided by Grace

from the vending machine at work or snuck into the conference room after the sales meetings to grab a leftover bagel. Top Ramen, peanut butter, and popcorn were staples in my life for many years. I now look back and think about how unhealthy I ate at that time. Fortunately, at twenty-four years old, your body can metabolize that type of diet, but not for long.

I took the job at Q101, desperate to make more income, and steering even further away from my true passion and purpose. At least at WXRT, I had mentors and coworkers who cared about me and saw me for me, and I could be myself around them. This was not the case at Q101. The decision to change jobs solely for the money was a huge lesson for me as I followed my hunger for financial freedom but ignored any early signs and my intuition that I was taking a wrong turn.

I knew in my gut from the first interview with my new boss that this was not going to be a good move, but I was so riddled with fear of not having enough money that I did it anyway. I convinced myself of all the reasons (in my head, not my heart) that this was the right move. The station was only three miles from my apartment, so my commute would be significantly easier. I would be working in the heart of the city, with tons of energy, excitement, and places to eat (and maybe now with my increased salary, I could afford to go out for lunch). The station was in the Merchandise Mart, a gigantic and gorgeous building set just to the north of the Chicago River.

But, most importantly, my office was closer to Charles, and I knew it would be easier for us to meet for lunch when we both could get away. My direct boss was a young sales manager who had not been in his role for very long. It wouldn't take long to learn he had a horrible temper. I often witnessed him having full-blown arguments with members of the sales staff in the middle of the office. He was volatile and angry, but because this was still the mid-1990s, he could get away with speaking to staff members that way.

If I remember correctly, we had a staff of all women, and it was a difficult environment to be in for my first sales position. This would never have happened at WXRT. The staff there were family, and they took care of one another. This was an entirely different environment, and I would get my first taste of what real corporate America could be like.

It's amazing to think how different times are now compared to then. You had to have thick skin and know how to navigate office politics in those days. I was so young and naïve, and I did not have the ability to manage all that was coming at me.

Within the first three months of working there, I experienced my first of what would become several years of massive anxiety attacks. I felt so alone, like no one truly had my back. I didn't like my new boss; honestly, I was afraid of him (he reminded me a lot of my dad when he got angry), but I was afraid to speak up for myself.

At least until one day when I couldn't control myself. I couldn't hold back after I witnessed how he treated the other young women in my office, and when he reprimanded me after I lost a small piece of business (that's what we called it when you had an opportunity to close a deal). I let him have it. Those old feelings of standing up for myself when my dad would yell at me came rushing back, and I had no way of controlling them.

When I was brought into the general sales manager's office (my boss's boss) for being insubordinate, I thought I was going to be fired on the spot. I admired her so much; she was everything I wanted to be: strong, confident, beautiful, extremely successful, and she had climbed her way up the ladder at that company from receptionist to running the entire sales department.

She was also calm and cool. When I sat down in front of her desk, I was trembling, and I knew she sensed how scared I was. Her energy was almost statuesque, as if she were there, but not entirely there. To this day, I don't know what she was truly thinking, if she wanted to reprimand me or congratulate me for standing up for myself. But again, it was the mid-1990s, and times were very different.

Guided by Grace

She was polite and didn't scold me, but she did let me know that I would need to make it work with my manager if I wanted to keep my job. I needed the job, so I sucked it up for as long as I could. I hated it there. I made one friend, Allison, who sat on the other side of the cubicle from me. She was the only person I really ever spoke to in that office. Allison had worked at Q101 for not much longer than I had, and although she didn't like our boss, she was much more controlled than I was. I would go out on sales calls to bars, restaurants, and shops all over Chicago and the surrounding areas, trying to get anyone who owned a business to advertise on the radio station.

I found myself in a lot of uncomfortable situations in back rooms of bars and auto shops, and while the company gave us a cell phone, I never felt safe. I remember thinking, I could disappear during one of these meetings and no one would ever know what happened to me. That went on for months and months. That time in my life was all about work and Charles. I had very little time with my other girlfriends, and as we were coming up on our third year in Chicago, each of my friends from college moved away.

Jen and her boyfriend decided to move home to Los Angeles, Stacy moved to St. Louis with her boyfriend, and Natasha moved to Rhode Island with her new boyfriend. I had to get an apartment by myself because Charles and I were not ready to move in together. I found a studio apartment in Old Town, right next to the infamous Second City. While it was a little further north of work, I was still close enough to Charles's apartment, so it was easy for me to catch a cab and be there within a few minutes.

After my girlfriends left, I felt truly isolated. I didn't like living alone, and I threw myself even further into my relationship. Charles and I did everything together; we were practically living together by then, as I hated sleeping by myself at my apartment and Charles liked being at his place. Many days, I can remember waking up early, before the sunrise, because I didn't have enough clothes at his place, and taking a cab back to my studio apartment in the frigid cold to get ready for work. I was so consumed by our relationship that I didn't realize how unhealthy it was.

Since I hated my job and hated living alone, the only piece of happiness I had was when I was with him. He made me feel safe, and we loved exploring the city together. He was adventurous and loved to take road trips and do exciting things. We often went to his parents' home in Indiana to spend time with them, and we would ride his snowmobiles in the country behind their home for hours. We spent weekends with my friend from WXRT, Karen, and her husband at their lake house in Michigan, and it seemed like our relationship was going to last a lifetime.

We were living the dream, until we weren't. About the time I was getting used to my girlfriends being gone, I found out Charles was seeing a woman behind my back, someone he had dated off and on for years. Their relationship was a strange and twisted one that had apparently been going on for some time.

One morning, when we were both getting ready for work, she showed up at his apartment. Charles was in the shower, so I answered the door, and there she was. We stared at each other for what seemed like several minutes, and even though I had never met her, I knew exactly who she was. She was significantly older than me (and Charles), and I was immediately intimidated. I was about twenty-six years old at this point, and this scenario was bringing up a familiar pain in my gut.

Even though I could stand up to my boss and my own father, this was uncharted territory. I went into the bathroom, opened the shower curtain, looked Charles dead in the eye, and said, "Sharon's here."

Then I stormed to the bedroom, grabbed as many of my things as I could carry, looked her in the eye and said, "Don't worry, you can have him to yourself, I'm leaving." Charles chased me down the hallway in a towel as I furiously pounded on the elevator button.

Luckily, it opened just as he got to the elevator, and I let it slowly close between us as I stared at him with tears pouring down my face. It was

Guided by Grace

like something out of a Hollywood romantic drama. I couldn't believe this was happening.

That next morning, I called in sick and stayed in bed all day. Charles came to my apartment, but I wouldn't let him in. Finally, after several phone calls and a huge bouquet of red roses arrived at my apartment the next day, I decided to give him another chance. I took a cab to his apartment without letting him know I was coming over.

When I arrived at his apartment front door, something told me to use the key he had given me and not knock to alert him that I was there. I didn't fully trust him anymore, and I wanted to believe that I could just walk in and he would be there alone, ready to embrace me.

I put the key into the lock and slowly turned the knob. As the door opened, I walked in and saw him sitting in the living room on the couch, staring down at the glass coffee table in front of him. There, on the coffee table, was a handgun. I froze. I had never seen a handgun before, and the picture of him sitting there with his eyes glassy and red is etched in my mind forever.

I ran over to him and hugged him. I told him I loved him and that we would figure this all out. He was relieved that I was there and had the instinct to come over. To this day, I don't know if he would have taken his own life, or if that was even why the handgun was sitting there. I was afraid to ask. I have never been so scared in my whole life.

I didn't realize until that moment all that he had going on inside. He was so alive and confident on the outside, yet clearly troubled. I stayed with him, and in some twisted way, my young ego trusted that he loved me if he was willing to take his own life if I didn't stay with him.

The truth is, it wasn't about me at all, but at the time, I didn't have the maturity, wisdom, or life experience to see what was really going on. I wanted to see and believe what *I* wanted him to be and never allowed myself to see who he really was or what he was dealing with. I was caught up in the idea of what I thought our relationship was, and I wasn't willing to see the truth. Once again, I had chosen to make a situation in a relationship mean something about me when it wasn't about me at all. If we do not allow ourselves to see the truth, our subconscious mind, or ego, will make something up. I made his words and actions mean something about *me* when in reality, they had far more to do with what he was carrying inside. It's so easy to let our egos twist things, convincing us that someone's behavior reflects our worth, when really, it often reflects their own inner struggles.

Many people, especially men, are conditioned to appear strong and stoic; they don't feel safe admitting their insecurities. So instead, they project. They create a story that deflects from their own pain or fear, turning the focus onto others.

When we don't recognize what's happening, we can internalize that story as our truth when it was never about us at all. It wasn't until I stepped back and got honest with myself that I could finally see it for what it was. That relationship became one of my greatest teachers because it revealed how often I abandoned my own inner knowing to make someone else feel comfortable. I realized I had been trying to earn love by being who I *thought* they needed, instead of honoring who I truly was.

Can you think of a time or a situation when you felt like someone in your life made you feel a certain way, and you allowed yourself to accept what they were saying or projecting onto you?

The truth is, no one can *make* you feel anything, and I know understanding that is easier said than done. But you do have a choice to feel how you want to feel, or to allow someone to project their feelings onto you. Their words and thoughts are just that, their own words and thoughts. They have no bearing on you at all.

If you are being manipulated into acting or being a certain way, you will know because it doesn't feel good. It's an underlying pang in your gut that tells you something is wrong, even if you can't put your finger on it.

This is not a healthy dynamic in a relationship. When you're being manipulated by someone who is projecting their feelings onto you, it can feel like standing in a fog—confused, disoriented, and doubting your own instincts. You start questioning your reality because their version of the story is so confidently delivered, even though something deep inside you whispers that it doesn't feel right. There's a subtle push and pull, like you're constantly adjusting yourself to keep the peace or avoid conflict.

You may feel responsible for their moods, walking on eggshells to avoid setting them off. Over time, their projection becomes a weight you carry, a narrative you didn't write but somehow start to believe. That's the true danger: not just in what they're saying or doing, but in how it slowly chips away at your trust in yourself. Manipulation isn't always loud or obvious; it's often quiet, disguised as concern, blame, or even love.

But underneath, it's about control. I was so afraid to leave Charles at this point, not only for fear of his safety, but because I had been hurt so badly in my previous relationship that I didn't want to go through that pain again. I allowed the fear and uncertainty of being alone to overpower my inner knowing and truth.

The craziest thing was that, with Charles, I felt compelled to protect him. Even though I still wondered if he was cheating on me, everything inside of me kicked in to protect him, not myself. I continued for several more months to create a sense of security in our relationship, but I was feeling anything but.

As time went on, there was an underlying fear that I couldn't escape. My loneliness continued, and my desperation for my relationship to go back to the way it was, and the survival of my job consumed me. With each passing day, the reasons why I lived in Chicago became less and less clear. It wasn't until a fateful morning when I started throwing up while getting ready for work that everything changed.

I was seven weeks pregnant. How did this happen? I had been on birth control pills since I was eighteen. I called my friend, Stacy, and that weekend I flew down to St. Louis to spend time with her. We sat in her apartment all weekend, listening to CDs and talking. I was trying to figure out my life. I hadn't even told Charles yet. I was too scared, knowing there was a good chance this could trigger him to respond in a way that I wasn't prepared for, and I wasn't strong enough at the time to face any of it. I didn't know what I wanted. I wanted it to go away, for everything to go away.

One of the most difficult things about life is that what you perceive your life to be and what the Universe and God have planned for you are often two very different things. No matter how hard you push for something to work, to go your way, or to control the outcome, if it's not what God has planned for you, there's no controlling it.

When you can recognize that everything that happens to you is actually happening for you, you take your power back. These challenges and often horrible circumstances are what you need to build the resilience and strength to grow and become the person you are designed to be. It's difficult to see at the time, but you will have wisdom and perspective the next time something challenging, scary, or downright awful happens to you or someone you care about.

You have a choice to shift your perspective, to ask yourself, *What is this situation trying to teach me?* and *What does God want me to do with this lesson?* It's easier said than done, believe me, I know. I am not sitting here writing this, thinking this is a simple shift in perspective.

It takes practice, especially if you've been through a life-changing incident that is completely beyond your control. It takes a while to deal with the fear, pain, and overwhelm, but the point is not to stay in that place for too long. Once you can get through the initial pain and fear, try to step outside of yourself and shift your view from being a victim of your situation to being the victor.

How can you change that narrative to create more power for yourself by choosing to look at it from the perspective of God's purpose for you? Your answer to that may need a bit to sink in, and don't worry, we will come back to this later, but if you feel compelled to stop and journal about this, ask yourself, *Is this situation trying to teach me something or guide me in a different direction?*

Now, I'm not sure if I can say that this pregnancy was a breadcrumb toward the path I was meant to follow at that point, but looking back on it, it certainly was the catalyst for me to switch direction in a profound way.

When I landed back in Chicago from my weekend with Stacy in St. Louis, it was late on Sunday evening. I took a cab straight to Charles's apartment and, fortunately, he was there, alone. I didn't have any idea what I was going to walk into since I had given him no information about where I had been or when I was coming back.

The doorman knew me so well, he just waved hello, and I went straight to the elevator. As scared as I was, I knew I couldn't wait any longer to tell Charles what was going on. I told him, but to be honest, I don't remember at all how he first responded to the news that I was pregnant. I have completely blocked it out.

I only remember that the following day, during lunch, he took me to Planned Parenthood in downtown Chicago. As we sat in the waiting room, I remember feeling so alone and scared. I did not know what to expect. When they called my name, I looked back for some reassurance from Charles, but he couldn't even look at me. I knew he was struggling too, but I didn't really know what he was feeling.

The crazy thing is, you would've thought we were teenagers, kids with no means of supporting a baby, or not ready to get married. But I was twenty-six, and he was almost thirty years old. We both had good-paying jobs by then, and there was no external reason why we couldn't have a baby. If he had asked me to marry him, I would have said yes, but after what you have just read about all that we had going on in our lives, this was a less-than-ideal situation to bring a baby into, much less to start a marriage. Talk about a recipe for disaster. But at that time, with my limited self-awareness and maturity, I would have done anything to save my relationship, my baby, and my future. I just couldn't see beyond that moment.

As the nurse took me down the long, cold hallway to the examination room, I remember feeling like I was coming out of my skin, that almost uncontrollable feeling of wanting to run in the other direction was literally coming up from deep inside me. This was a real fight-or-flight situation, yet I felt paralyzed.

After the ultrasound was done, and I was taken to another room to sit and wait for the doctor, I started uncontrollably sobbing before the nurse even left the room. She consoled me, and I will never forget what she said next. She whispered, "Is this your decision, honey?" I looked up at her with the biggest sense of relief and responded through sobs, "I'm not sure." She then walked me into a small, comfortable sitting room close to the larger waiting room. A few minutes later, she returned with Charles. He looked at me, confused, and I told him, "I'm not ready to make this decision."

There was nothing he could say. The nurse stared at him as if she were telepathically scolding him and said, "This isn't your decision to make; it's hers." I truly think that nurse changed my life in many ways. She gave me the path to power over my own decisions.

Had she not asked me if I was okay, I would have likely gone through with a decision I wasn't prepared to make, and there would have been an entire list of consequences resulting from that decision afterward that would likely have taken me down even further in the direction of loneliness, desperation, and depression.

She gave me my power back, and I believe that she was a guardian angel sent to me to protect my future and the future of my purpose in life. God knew at that time what I needed and intervened.

The car ride back to my office was made in dead silence. No radio, no talking, just dead quiet. I will never forget getting out of his car in front of my office building; I turned around to close the door, and Charles said, "I'm not ready to be a father."

Guided by Grace

My heart was broken. Almost three years of my life had been spent with this person, whom I thought I knew. I believed he loved me, and I hoped that at least he would want to have the conversation about what it would look like to have a baby.

But fear, and I'm sure the internal awareness he had that he was in no shape to be a father at that point, were what kept him from expressing what he truly felt. And even though I knew we were facing so many issues between us, I just wanted him to say that he loved me and we would figure it out together.

That day after work, I went back to my lonely apartment and called my mom. I was so afraid of what she would say. I hadn't told anyone except Charles and Stacy. My mom surprised me. She wasn't upset; she was, of course, concerned (although I do remember her saying at one point over the phone that she wondered when this would happen).

She told me to fly home, and we would figure it out together. I called my boss the next day and told him I had to go back to LA for an emergency health issue and would be out for the rest of the week.

Once I was home in California, I finally felt safe. I knew I could take the time I needed to think about my situation and what I truly wanted. Thank God for my mom and her new life (both my parents remarried not long after I went back to school) and perspective, because she was happy and clear-minded enough to know how to handle it.

I'm not saying that if she were still married to my dad, she wouldn't have handled it the same way, but she was a different person now. She had developed courage and strength that I had not witnessed before.

The truth is, even at twenty-six, I wasn't ready to have a baby, and definitely not on my own without the father's support. Here's the toughest part: I had always imagined that if I ever got pregnant, there would be excitement, joy, and a clear vision for the future. But when it actually happened, none of that was there.

Jennifer Mentesana

I remember sitting in my parents' home, wondering how I could possibly do this. I was living in a city I didn't love, working a job that felt meaningless, with a boyfriend who was likely cheating on me and who had made it clear he wasn't ready to be a father. I kept searching for a connection to this pregnancy, to a sense of purpose or direction for my life, but I couldn't find it. It felt as if I had stepped into a fog with no way forward.

This story isn't about politics or opinions. It was deeply personal—between me, my mom, and God. If I had felt, even for a moment, that God wanted me to move in one direction, I would have followed it with every ounce of strength I had. But instead, I was invited into a season of prayer, stillness, and listening.

My mom and I cried together, prayed together, and asked for clarity without anyone else's voice or opinion but God's. I stayed quiet, even keeping Charles at a distance because I needed to hear only one voice in the midst of the noise—God's.

What I learned in that moment was the power of trusting my own connection with God above anyone else's expectations. People, sometimes even entire religions, will try to tell you what's right for your life. But only you can hear God's whisper for your soul. His voice never comes from fear or pressure; it comes from love, purpose, and a knowing that transcends logic.

And so, I made the decision to place everything in His hands. I didn't have the answers then, and I certainly don't have them all now. But what I do know is that God met me there—in the confusion, in the tears, in the waiting, and He guided me through one of the most difficult seasons of my life. That experience reshaped me. It gave me clarity about the kind of life I wanted for myself and the kind of love and family I would create one day.

When I returned to Chicago and went on with life as normally as possible, things between Charles and me were different. I just couldn't get back to feeling the way I had felt about him for those past few years.

Guided by Grace

We were on again, off again, and I wasn't sure if he was still seeing that woman behind my back.

I felt so lonely and insecure, and one night I went out with some friends from work and saw him out with his friends. We got into a big fight, and I went back to my apartment and drank at least a bottle of red wine by myself while talking on the phone to my friends back home.

I woke up the next morning, passed out in a large pool of red wine vomit, and I realized my life was headed for a really bad turn if I didn't get my act together.

By the time summer rolled around, I had lost hope for any real reconciliation with Charles and whatever life I had left in Chicago. I quit my hated job and moved back to LA. Charles and I agreed we would try to stay in touch and salvage what we could long-distance. I think both of us were afraid to end it completely, but we knew it wouldn't last.

Reclaiming your power begins the moment you stop explaining yourself to someone who's not truly listening and start honoring the voice within that's been quietly asking for more. When I finally chose to leave, it wasn't because I had all the answers or felt completely ready; it was because I had *enough* clarity to know that staying was costing me too much. I had betrayed myself long enough. Walking away wasn't easy. It rarely is. But it was the most sacred act of self-respect I could offer myself. I wasn't leaving to punish or to prove anything. I was leaving to return home to who I truly was. And in doing so, I began to heal, to hear myself again, and to remember that love should never come at the expense of my peace, power, or truth.

Jennifer Mentesana

Have you ever found yourself in a relationship where you felt responsible for someone else's emotions or began questioning your own reality because of their words or behavior?

Take a moment to reflect: Were there times when you silenced your intuition just to keep the peace or maintain the connection? Spend some time journaling about how that dynamic made you feel emotionally, physically, and spiritually. What parts of yourself did you quiet or abandon in order to stay? Most importantly, what would it look like to begin reclaiming those parts now?

Be honest, and give yourself grace. This is your space to begin unravelling what is not yours to carry.

Chapter 7
Healing

*"The soul always knows what to do to heal itself.
The challenge is to silence the mind."*
–Caroline Myss

L iving back at home in LA, I felt somewhat at peace again for the first time in a long time. This was where I belonged, and the long journey of life in the Midwest, after eight years, was officially over.

I slowly started to get back on my feet and look for a job. I was living between both of my parents' homes, and both of them had new spouses. I felt so uncomfortable and displaced going back and forth between their homes, neither of which felt like my own.

I spent many nights on Stacy's couch in her apartment in Beverly Hills (she had left St. Louis and her boyfriend behind). She had a new boyfriend, and although we all got along great, it was a one-bedroom apartment, and I was starting to overstay my welcome. I waited tables again until I could figure out a plan to get another job in media, obviously not aware enough to realize that I needed to spend some time going inward to figure out what I truly wanted my life to be.

Still in survival mode, now almost five years out of college, you would think that I would have figured out that the path I was headed down was not working. But once again, the fear of not having financial security consumed me.

I wanted the freedom to live on my own, or at least with a roommate, so I could create a home and a life for myself. Almost twenty-eight years old, I was starting to panic about my future. While I knew I could always stay with my Grandma Audrey, my Grandpa Walt was still alive, and he was suffering from early symptoms of ALS.

I didn't want to put any more on their plate, so I would visit for long hours to keep my grandma company while Grandpa Walt slept, but I would always go back to my mom's, dad's, or Stacy's. The only way I could see myself being able to afford to move to my own place was to go back into media sales, where I at least had a few years of experience and could get a steady salary and benefits.

I started applying for jobs, including at Turner Network Television as a TV sales rep. I got down to the final interview, and it was between me and one other candidate. I had stupidly given my previous boss at Q101 as a reference (I was so clueless, I didn't realize I didn't have to put down my previous employer as a reference). When the executive I interviewed with called me to tell me I didn't get the job, she was kind enough to tell me that I was their first choice, but because my previous employer had given me a bad review, they didn't feel like they could move forward. I learned my lesson there. Never use someone you don't respect or have a good relationship with as a reference.

Fortunately for me, the next opportunity was a turning point that carried me through the next few years. Not long after I was turned down for the position at Turner, Charles referred me to a media sales rep firm that represented radio stations all over the country. The radio station where Charles worked was represented by this LA firm, and I interviewed and was hired on the spot. (I know this is cliché, but so much of life is not about what you know, but who you know and, more importantly, your ability to connect with others.)

I connected right away with the sales manager and the rest of the team. It was a great place to work. The office was filled with lots of young, fun, and energetic salespeople in their mid-twenties working long hours and playing hard after work.

I worked at least twelve-hour days; I was expected to be in the office before 7:30 a.m. since our stations on the East Coast had already been in the office for several hours. Our west coast stations were still in the office at 6:30 p.m., so we were expected to be available should any of our station GMs (general managers) or NSMs (national sales managers) need to get in touch with us (cell phones and mobile offices were not yet a big thing).

Most evenings, we would leave the office around 7 p.m., grab drinks with clients or each other, and not get home until 10 or 11 p.m., and then turn around and do it all again the next day. It was definitely a young person's career. I think in those days, we were out at night in LA at least three out of five work nights.

Many mornings, I came into the office exhausted and hungover, and I would lie on my boss's couch in his office until the phones started ringing. He never minded. It was just the business we were in. Work hard, play hard. And it was expected! Going out for drinks with clients or the team was not optional. It didn't matter if you needed sleep or had a boyfriend or other plans. It was considered "part of the job."

The sales team did everything together, and I even remember my boss telling me once that I would be lucky to have a social life outside of this place. I was finally able to move out of the many crash pads I had been living in and move into a house with some of my high school friends. As much as I loved staying with Stacy and her new boyfriend, they needed their space, and I needed sleep!

Jennifer Mentesana

My friends Jolee, Tory, and I moved into a cute condo in Redondo Beach that Jolee purchased, and it was perfect. We all had our own rooms and a cute place to call home. My friend, and Jolee's sister, Leslee, bought the condo next door, and we were a big, happy family for the next couple of years. It was truly the happiest I had been in a long time.

Charles and I were speaking less and less, although he once came out to LA for a work trip, and I would see him since our company represented his station. I had started dating "Tom," a guy who worked in my office building in one of the other rep firms within the company. He was fun, funny, and a great distraction from all I had been through the previous year. And because he worked in the building, and we were all a big family, it was easy to see each other since we were all always together.

By the time Charles came to LA for his work trip, I had been in my relationship with Tom for about four months. Charles was so happy to see me; it was the first time we had seen each other since I left Chicago almost a year before.

Part of me felt sick to my stomach when I saw him, yet part of me wanted to grab him and kiss him. It was the strangest feeling. He came to my office when he first arrived, and I didn't know how to act.

In that moment (I mean, you can't make this stuff up), Tom walked in to talk to me. They looked at each other, and I think they both knew immediately who the other was. Charles didn't know I was seeing someone, but I think he could tell by the energy that was flying around the room that Tom was more than a coworker.

After work that evening, Charles and the rest of my team went out for drinks. Charles was visibly upset, but I acted like nothing was wrong, even though my heart was being ripped out of my chest. We were with my team, and Charles was our "client." I needed to keep things professional, so I never tried to explain anything or even talk to him about

Guided by Grace

our personal relationship. It had been over for me since I moved back to LA, but we never really ended it.

That was the last time I ever saw him. Charles went back to his hotel that night and flew back to Chicago the next day. Although we tried to connect a few times after that, it just never happened. I once went back to Chicago with Stacy to visit him and my friend, Karen, and he told me he couldn't meet up with me the night I got there because he had other plans. That was it. We never spoke again.

As I was writing this book in November 2024, I got a call from my friend, Karen, from Chicago, telling me that Charles had passed away at fifty-seven. He never married, although he had a few other relationships over the years since we dated. He lived and worked in media in Chicago for almost thirty years, and from what I know, had a fantastic career and a life full of great friends and family.

He passed away in his home alone, and I never got to tell him I was sorry for what happened between us. Even though our relationship was over, a part of me felt tied to him in an inexplicable way. I never had any regrets about anything, but I did feel very emotional when I got the news that he had passed.

About a week after his death, I had the most incredible dream. I dreamed I flew to Chicago and went to his memorial service, which was at one of his favorite media hangouts. When I walked through the door, he was sitting at the table, laughing and telling stories with everyone. I was stunned. I walked over to him and asked him why he was there and what was going on. He told me he couldn't leave without saying goodbye!

For the rest of the night, we were side by side, telling stories about our lives since we last saw each other. Then, we turned to look out the window, and some kids were playing out in front. It was *my kids*! My boys, Nicolas and Andrew.

He asked to meet them, and when I called them in to introduce them, he asked my son, Nicolas about baseball. He somehow knew that my son's passion is baseball, and he told him stories about his years playing in college. My dream was so vivid and so special. He then turned and smiled at me, and we walked out together. The moment before I woke up, the last thing I saw was his crystal blue eyes and long blond eyelashes staring into mine. It was incredible.

No matter what you believe in this life, I'm here to tell you that we are all spiritual beings having a human experience. There are no boundaries between this lifetime and the next or this world and the one beyond; the only boundary is what you believe.

People come into your life for a reason, a season, or a lifetime, so the saying goes. I'm not great at goodbyes, and definitely not when someone comes into my life with such impact and connection. Those are usually the hardest ones to let go.

But if by now you haven't grasped the underlying message of this book, I'm not doing a very good job of writing it! The Universe and, more importantly, God, have a plan for your life. Whether you accept that or not.

The truth is, it is up to you to follow the breadcrumbs and do the work to keep moving forward. We all get sidetracked or even stuck and potentially go down a path that isn't meant for us. But there are beautiful lessons in that path, preparing you for what's to come.

If you choose to go through it, through the pain and the muck to reach the other side, the lesson is beautiful and will change your life for the better. However, if you choose to remain stuck, resisting the lesson and the purpose within the pain, you may find yourself either trapped in blame, dwelling on circumstances or those you hold responsible, or suppressing it so deeply that, over time, it festers and resurfaces even more painfully.

At the end of the day, your life is up to you, no matter what happens to you. You can blame your parents, your boss, your exes, or even God or the Universe, but only you have the power to make the change necessary to live the life you were born to live.

Guided by Grace

I believe we choose our lessons before we are born. It's as if God gives us a blank slate and says, "Okay, what lessons and purpose do you want for this lifetime?" You choose the parents, circumstances, and even the relationships you are going to experience before you are born.

There are no accidents. You innately know that these are the lessons you are here to learn, to become your fullest potential in the eyes of God. He is preparing you to become more like him—wise, completely loving and forgiving, and ultimately free of human flaws.

As we go through life as human beings, we unexpectedly pull in the lessons we have chosen to learn, and it is up to us to learn them and continue on the path toward God and His purpose for us, and what we have chosen.

The ironic thing is, and this might be controversial to some, I believe what we have been taught (by traditional religion) about what God wants from and for us is not necessarily true. God wants us to make mistakes and learn from them. He doesn't want us to live in this robotic state of obedience, doing all the right things, saying all the right things, and never taking risks.

Organized religion created that narrative, not God. God wants us to have the whole human experience so we can learn. Of course, there are limitations, and most people know those limitations deep within their souls.

Most of us know the difference between right and wrong. Even a two-year-old usually doesn't need to be told it's wrong to hit someone. They may have the instinct to hit in response to something they feel threatened by to protect themselves, but being driven to do so doesn't feel good. We all know instinctively at a young age what feels good and what feels bad. Love feels good; anger and hate feel bad. Some are more inclined to engage in what we consider "bad" behavior, but consider the possibility that it may be a lesson they chose to learn before they were born.

There are those who have completely lost their way and do not operate with any connection to their higher power; thus, they do horrific things and continue to make choices that take them far away from the life they were intended to live. Even these people can get back on track, which usually comes with a deep spiritual awakening and reconnection to God's purpose for them.

Often, there is a giant breadcrumb that creates such an impact in their lives that they are compelled to completely turn their lives around and may even go on a mission to help others with the same challenges they had. Think about recovering alcoholics who have ruined their lives, destroyed their families, and everything they have.

Usually, the way they get back on track is by connecting with their higher power and helping others who are going through the same thing they did. It's the same for criminals. When they choose to reconnect with God, and their divine path is revealed, they can grow and evolve into who they were meant to be.

There is an age-old debate about *nature* versus *nurture*. As a parent of three children, one now an adult and two teenagers, I am more convinced than ever that these little souls were born into this world with everything they needed to become who they were meant to be.

Of course, parenting, education, and life experiences influence and shape them, but who they will become has more to do with God, their lessons, and their path than anything else. Sorry, moms and dads out there who think they are going to raise their child to become exactly who they want and expect them to be, but our children already possess the strengths, talents, and purpose deep within them.

Our job is to support them on the path to their true purpose and destiny, to become the purest, most actualized version of what God created them to be. I have two boys living at home, and at the time I am writing this book, they are fifteen and thirteen, and they could not be more different from each other.

Guided by Grace

They were completely different babies, completely different kids, and they are becoming completely different adults. Their environment is shaping them to be kind, respectful, feel loved, safe, and challenged to be their best, but in the end, that's all we can do as parents.

No amount of helicopter parenting is going to change who they will become; if anything, it will do more harm than good because if you are a helicopter parent (no offense if you are, but this is the truth), you are keeping them from becoming who they are designed to be. If anything, it may stifle their growth or cause them to rebel.

Now, please understand that in no way am I suggesting that you let your kids do whatever they want, believe whatever they want, and go hog wild out into the world; it's your choice as a parent how you want to shape them.

However, I have seen it many times myself that the more parents push their children to do or be something they don't want, the more it backfires. Most importantly, we are taking away important lessons from them if we meddle too much in their path. Our job is to keep them safe, give them love, and guide them through life. Our job as parents is not to force our desires or our own needs onto them.

I am a firm believer in connecting with your children to truly find what makes them tick. Not just what makes them happy, but truly makes them come alive. It's the same for adults: Nurture the gifts and talents that God has given you to share with the world.

These are instinctively inside of every human being and are meant to be expressed. Nurture those innate talents and passions, encourage them in others, and see your children and others for who they really are, because when a child (and adult) feels seen, they will have the confidence to take on the world!

Jennifer Mentesana

Now take a moment to write in your journal about your inner knowing of who you truly are. By this point, you have been journaling long enough to be more connected to your intuition and to your higher power. What does this chapter reveal to you about the lessons you have experienced in this lifetime, and have you truly learned from them?

Chapter 8
The Illusion

"We do not see things as they are, we see them as we are."
–Anaïs Nin

For the next year of my life working in media in LA and dating Tom, I was finally getting back on track. (Or at least I should say I was financially stable and no longer grieving.) My heavy life with Charles was behind me, and I started to picture my future again. I thrived at work, loved my new home with my friends, and Tom and I lived the life of successful twenty-somethings in LA and all that came with it.

We went out on the weekends to all of the LA hotspots, dined at the best restaurants, and went to the best parties. We hung out with celebrities and partied all night after working all day.

While most of my friends were starting to get engaged and settle down, I was just ramping up, enjoying all that came along with being a young professional with a successful career. I was finally feeling as though things were looking up for me. It had been a long road since my parents' divorce, moving to Chicago, and struggling to survive on my own, not to mention what I went through with Charles. I was relieved to not be worried about anything for the first time in years.

Things went along like this for at least a year, and we started to travel all over the country, going to our friends' weddings and essentially living a life that wasn't rooted in reality.

We went back to Tom's hometown often and stayed with his family. I adored his mom. She was so good to me, and I truly cherished the time we spent with them. His friends back home were great, so fun and full of life, just like him. That time in our lives was one giant party.

Tom proposed to me over the holiday season in 1999 in a very romantic fashion. He flew me to San Francisco, and we stayed at a fabulous hotel on Nob Hill. We went to one of the best restaurants in town, then to see the *Nutcracker* at the opera house, and then he took me back to our hotel room, where he proposed. I was so shocked, I really wasn't expecting it, even as I recall it today. I was so swept away in the moment that we both cried and laughed and called our parents and friends to tell them the news.

When we got back to LA, the planning began. We were going to have a November wedding the following year. I knew everything that I wanted, and I dove headfirst into the excitement that comes with planning a wedding.

Within a few months, we had the date set, the church, the reception, our wedding party, and even my dress had been decided. My best friend, Jen, was getting married that summer, and we were so busy between her wedding and mine that I hardly remember anything else from that year. It was a year of constant wedding showers, engagement parties, and bachelor and bachelorette weekends. It was all about the parties, and there was little time to think about the actual marriage Tom and I would have.

Our wedding was absolutely beautiful. We got married on a crisp November day in my hometown at the Neighborhood Church, a 1920s

Guided by Grace

Spanish estate that had been repurposed as the town's first church. The pews looked out to the ocean just beyond the terrace, and the altar felt as though you were in an old Spanish castle somewhere.

It was a fairy tale. I can hardly remember the vows we took that day, but I remember Tom's face, so proud and happy, and I, too, was happy. We danced and partied at the reception afterward and stayed at a beautiful hotel right on the beach for our wedding night. We ordered cheeseburgers from room service and stayed up drinking champagne until the sun came up. It was truly magical. After ten sun-soaked days in Tahiti for our honeymoon, we came back to LA and settled into married life.

The hard part was, now that we were married, the partying and Hollywood life we had been living didn't feel right. Within a year of us getting married, we decided to make a change and remove ourselves from the Hollywood scene. We settled on moving to North County San Diego, close to one of Tom's best friends, and Tom took a job at a radio station downtown.

I decided to take a break from media, ready for a little less hustle and bustle and prepared to settle into a more "traditional" role. At the time, it did not seem practical to pursue a demanding career in media if I was going to be a wife and homemaker. I had this vision of my life and what it was supposed to look like. I believed I wanted the white picket fence, the house in a good neighborhood on a hill, and everything that came with it. I had never imagined anything different for myself, and it never occurred to me that I might not live that life.

The truth is, I was not really connected to what that life actually meant. I could picture the outside of it, but I never stopped to ask what I was truly seeking on the inside. What was the feeling I hoped those things would bring? It had not occurred to me to ask myself what I really wanted at the heart of it all. We must always ask, *What is the feeling I want from having the thing?* It is never really about the house, the car, the job, or even the person. It is about the feeling that comes from those experiences. At that stage of my life, I had not learned this yet, which is why I kept chasing money and financial security.

Jennifer Mentesana

I figured I would take my shot at becoming a Realtor so before we moved, I studied for my real estate license, passed the test, and we moved south the very next day. We thought this would be a good decision to create more reality and connection in our marriage and to allow ourselves to spend some much-needed time becoming husband and wife. It seemed like a perfectly practical and responsible decision, and I couldn't help but be excited about our new adventure.

For the first few months, it was great. I got a job with a high-end real estate company in Rancho Santa Fe, one of the most affluent areas of San Diego. I worked for an established realtor, helping him pull listings for clients, putting marketing materials together, and taking notes at sales meetings.

I was meeting new people and being exposed to some incredible businesspeople and entrepreneurs who lived in the area. I would prepare the listings, getting the homes ready to be shown to potential buyers, and it all felt very glamorous. I even got to take some clients out and show them properties. I thought I was on the path to a successful new career (yet even further from the path I was meant to go down).

Meanwhile, Tom was working downtown, and we would meet at home for dinner each night, further settling into married life. We cooked often, played tennis, and watched endless hours of TV. It didn't take long for our new, slower lifestyle to catch up with us.

About six months into our new life in San Diego, I started to get this nagging feeling in my gut. I couldn't pick up on what it was, and I pushed it down, telling myself it was just the reality of adjusting to change. (What I didn't want to see or accept was that this nagging feeling was actually a breadcrumb, telling me I was on the wrong path.)

As time went on at work, my boss got more interested in having me run his errands, which included taking his Mercedes to the car wash, picking up his dry cleaning, and cleaning out his garage.

Guided by Grace

I started to feel beholden to him, that if I dared say no, he would fire me on the spot. It was a twisted, uncomfortable dynamic, and I couldn't help but feel like I needed to get out of that situation.

It was at this time in life that I noticed this pattern I had with working for men. They either wanted me to date them, be their mistress, or control me. After a few more months of that behavior, I just quit on the spot. I didn't care enough about my job, or real estate for that matter, and I talked to Tom about taking some time off to figure out what to do.

This was around August 2001. Tom was busy with work, and I started to spend a lot of my time reading. I became really interested in self-help books and self-discovery. I was on a journey to figure out all that I had gone through since graduating from college, and where I stood in terms of the path of my life and career.

I knew then that I was lost, but I wasn't sure where to go with it. I figured, since I was married and Tom could provide for us for the short term, I would be able to take the time I needed to figure it out. I started to train for a marathon and became focused on really healing from the inside out for the first time in a long time, maybe ever.

There were periods when we would travel, hang out with friends, and go out and party, but most of the time I was alone, with my thoughts and space to think and learn more about myself and where I was in my personal journey. The month after I quit my real estate job, the world turned upside down. On the morning of September 11, 2001, I was sitting up in my bed watching the *Today* show when the scene of the second plane hitting the World Trade Center played out on television. Everyone who was alive then remembers where they were in that moment.

It was 8 a.m. on the West Coast, and Tom was getting ready for work. I screamed for him to come into the bedroom, and we both just sat there for what seemed like an eternity watching with disbelief. As the horrific scenes continued to play out, I will never forget what happened next.

Jennifer Mentesana

After about thirty minutes, Tom said, "Well, I've got to get to work." He kissed my forehead and left. In that moment, I knew there was something that didn't feel right, but I didn't allow myself to admit it for quite some time. I was shocked. I couldn't understand how he would want to go to work when our country was being attacked. It occurred to me that it was the first time he and I had witnessed something tragic happening together, as we had been living in this honeymoon phase and living the high life for so long, I didn't really know this side of him. It wasn't that his reaction was right or wrong; it was that it occurred to me that I didn't really know him because we had never gone through any sort of adversity together. Our move to San Diego had forced us to slow down and get to know each other from a different perspective.

Not long after 9/11, Tom told me he wanted to pursue his passion for motorsports, particularly NASCAR. He had been a fan all of his life, and he wanted to follow his passion for racing and use his experience in media sales to start a new business venture.

Of course, I was on board, as I thought this would be a great distraction for both of us and a new opportunity for us to learn and grow together as a couple. We dove headfirst into his new venture, and Tom found a young racecar driver who was looking for an opportunity to race in the Winston Cup series in Phoenix in a few months.

Tom hustled and found a sponsor to cover the costs for one race and to get this young driver into the lineup. It was so exciting, and to this day, I still remember arriving at the racetrack in Phoenix, connecting with the sponsors and meeting the other drivers and teams, and the excitement for what our future was to become took over. Not long after that race in Phoenix, we moved back to LA, where all our connections were, so that Tom could grow his business. I was relieved to go back, knowing that I would have my friends around to fill the void of loneliness and feelings I had in San Diego.

We moved to the most beautiful part of LA, the Pacific Palisades. (The entire community was ravaged in the devastating fires in January 2025, as I write this.) We found the cutest two-story apartment right off

Guided by Grace

Sunset Boulevard, only a mile from the ocean. I felt at peace there because I was home and could pour myself into our business and my social life.

Tom continued to build his company, go after sponsors, and fly to Charlotte and elsewhere to network and build his clientele.

He started traveling more on his own to different cities and races without me. I was still figuring out what I was going to do with my life and career, and pursuing anything that I could to find a path that would align with my passion and intuition.

I volunteered at several organizations and even took a job at the United Way for a period to explore nonprofit work. It was there that I learned to hone my public speaking skills as I went out to companies all over Los Angeles and spoke to teams about giving back to their communities. (This was a huge **breadcrumb** that I didn't realize at the time, but now I look back on it as an integral part of my journey.)

I took classes at night at UCLA in philanthropy and cause-related marketing. I began to explore my innate drive to become more than just a media salesperson. I wanted to make a difference somehow, but I didn't exactly know in what way.

By the end of that year, I was becoming emotionally disconnected from Tom. He was traveling, and when he was home, we partied with our friends. We went on hikes on the weekends when we didn't have plans, and I would try to talk to him about our future, searching for any way to create more connection between us.

One day, on our usual Sunday morning hike, I got this feeling in my gut that things were starting to fall apart. We were under a lot of stress financially, and I wanted to talk about anything that we could look forward to for some joy in our lives, but we were not in a good place. I knew I needed to get a job again quickly to help with the finances and offset some of the pressure he was feeling.

Jennifer Mentesana

Another fateful **breadcrumb** landed in my lap during one of my cause-related marketing classes at UCLA. As one of my assignments, I wrote a proposal for a marketing campaign in motorsports benefiting the Make-A-Wish Foundation. I was determined to make some sort of difference, but also benefit my husband's business somehow.

I had created a campaign that I thought was genius, and when a media professional came to speak to the class one evening, I knew it was divine intervention. Her name was Dannie-Mo, and I will never forget her. (If you are reading this, Dannie-Mo, you changed the trajectory of my life). She spoke about her purpose for making a difference through marketing and media. She worked at KCBS-FM in LA and was so passionate about her work that I could hardly contain myself when I listened to her talk.

Please make a mental (or literal) note about this before I go on with the story. Whenever you feel yourself almost coming out of your body with excitement or joy, pay attention to that. That is your intuition, and yes, a **breadcrumb**! That is God (or the Universe, again, whatever you believe) telling you this is your path. Whatever you do, don't (and it's almost impossible not to) dismiss this feeling and message. Follow it down the path of wherever it leads you because the path is guiding you to your true purpose.

Immediately after her talk, I went up to Dannie-Mo at the front of the classroom and introduced myself. I was literally coming out of my skin from excitement. I told her that I had this idea I wanted to present to her, and that I had been working in media and radio sales for most of my career.

We set up a time for coffee a week later and met at the Starbucks across from her office on Sunset Boulevard in Hollywood. I pitched her my campaign idea, and she loved the fact that I was creative and passionate about giving back.

The idea was to create an experience for children in the Make-A-Wish Foundation program to have the opportunity to ride along in a racecar with a NASCAR driver. The goal would be to find a sponsor to provide funding for the experience, and we would run a media campaign on the radio and through live promotions to create awareness. I thought it was genius, and apparently, Dannie-Mo thought so too because she took it to her boss at KCBS to present and landed me an interview.

I was excited about the interview, and although I would be working at a radio station again, this position would be more aligned with my passion for making a difference than with traditional media sales.

I got the job, but the first six months or so were uneventful. I went to work, sat at my desk, made phone calls the entire day, and prayed I would get some sort of response from any contact who might be interested in sponsoring the campaign I had created.

I was pretty quiet at work and didn't really talk to anyone, even though my desk was situated at the entrance of a giant room of cubicles with over a dozen salespeople. People walked by my desk, and I just kept my head down, trying to focus on closing my first deal. There was a lot of pressure to prove myself, and I was desperate to close my first deal to support Tom's motorsports marketing business.

About eight months into my employment at KCBS, my boss asked me to take an assessment. It was one of those personality tests, like Myers-Briggs, that indicate your strengths and weaknesses. I had participated in several of these types of exercises in my career, but usually it was a group assessment where I received training and an explanation of my core personality traits.

This assessment was given to me to figure out if I was really a good fit for this role. The findings of the assessment were spot on. The truth was (and it was finally there right in front of me, and it wasn't a shock) that I didn't have the strengths of a "typical" salesperson. The assessment showed that I had strengths in presentation and excellent communication skills, but the core values that were glaring were my desire to make a difference and the need to make an impact.

Jennifer Mentesana

These weren't exactly the strengths that a marketing sales manager is looking for on their team. I wanted to win, but not if it was not what was best for the client, their budget, or their goals. When my boss read the results to me, she acknowledged that these were strong qualities in a human being, but she didn't know what to do with me in terms of helping me hone my strengths to become a better salesperson.

I find it so ironic, because to this day, I still remember the immense feelings of failure from the outcome of that assessment. My whole career had been wrapped up in sales, and while there were times when I questioned what I was doing, I considered myself a salesperson.

I don't know why this came as such a shock. I had known what my true path was meant to be a decade before, but I chose to ignore those breadcrumbs to chase financial freedom. So many people who met me would say, "You would be great at sales!" But the truth is, I just loved connecting with people, learning what made them tick, and helping them fulfill that. How managers motivate teams is so different now than it was even back then in the early 2000s. Now we know that the stronger the relationships and authentic connections you create, the more successful you will become.

How you motivate people is about inspiring them to see their gifts and strengths and apply them to create opportunities. It's not about focusing on what's not working, but focusing on what can and will. It turns out I was a salesperson for a future generation that had not been created yet. I choose to believe, ahead of my time.

As I was writing this book, I was approached by someone who pitched me on a project. Because the pitch lacked heart and authenticity, and seemed more focused on closing the deal than on what was best for me, I chose to walk away. I do not like being sold to, and I do not like self-serving salespeople. I believe the best salespeople come from a place of service first, with a genuine value for true partnership and a win-win outcome, not simply skill at pressuring others into buying something they do not need or really want.

Guided by Grace

People want authenticity, real connection, and a mutual desire to make each other successful.

Anything other than that is not in alignment with the Universe and how it flows. I'm not saying that you won't be successful if you don't operate that way, but in my opinion, and what I have witnessed and learned over the years, your true path to wealth is so much more than just closing deals.

After receiving the assessment results and having that conversation with my manager, I felt deflated. I had spent years in a career that I was never going to be good at. The truth is that assessment allowed me to accept who I truly was, but it didn't change the fact that I needed to make money.

So again, I stuck with it, believing that if I just worked hard enough, it would all work out. I went on day by day, trying to close any deal at this point, not just the campaign I was so excited about. My purpose once again became survival, and was no longer about the passion for what I was there to do.

I was so disappointed because I had been working for almost a year to get that campaign off the ground, and I really believed it was going to happen. I truly believed that the moment in that UCLA classroom where I listened to Dannie-Mo speak was going to change my life. Little did I know it would, but not at all in the way I thought.

All while this was going on, my marriage was crumbling. There was very little joy in my life at home, only the occasional dinners we would host with Stacy and her husband, and a few of Tom's friends.

Our finances, my stress at work, and the travel and lifestyle of Tom's motorsports marketing company began to put even more strain on our relationship, and I started to feel a little more like a housekeeper than a wife. I remember calling my mom on several occasions and complaining about how I felt like a maid. She reminded me that I will feel like that a lot, especially when we have kids. I may have gone along with it for years, accepting it as my reality, but I had big dreams for my life, and at thirty-two years old, I already felt as if they were dying. The next step for us was to start a family, but that was the last thing I wanted at this time.

The life we had been living before we got married was a fantasy—parties and travel, high-end restaurants, and Hollywood hot spots. Our life now was so far from that, and the reality of how my marriage and my life with Tom were unfolding sank me into a deep depression. Many days, I lay in bed pretending to be sick so that I could sleep the day away and not feel anything.

I did my best to stay focused at work, but even that was difficult on most days. I started not caring how I looked, hardly wore makeup to work, and rarely styled my hair. (For many years, I got up an hour earlier just to blow-dry my hair for work.) For the first time in my adult life, I went to work with my hair wet, pulled back in a bun. I didn't care much about anything.

How did I get here? Here I was again, feeling disconnected, alone, and struggling at work—just as I had a few years before in Chicago with Charles. The difference was that I had been married for almost three years at this point, and things were as bleak as ever. I couldn't help but wonder if this was a pattern *I* was creating. I started pondering the fact that I was attracting relationships and certain dynamics for a specific reason. I realized I needed to look inward for the answers and understand why this was happening again. I spent a lot of time reading, journaling, and processing what I was feeling just as I had when we were living in San Diego the first year we were married.

That was the beginning of a journey that opened a whole new path and perspective for me. I began seeing a therapist, and one of my best friends, Kellie, who was a clinical psychologist (I will tell you more about her later, as her story is relevant), supported me emotionally through all of it.

Kellie referred me to a psychiatrist who prescribed some medication because my severe anxiety and depression were becoming debilitating.

Guided by Grace

I needed to work because I needed the job, but there were days I could hardly get out of bed because I felt so paralyzed from the situation I was in.

But most importantly, during that time, I was introduced to Mary Lee, a spiritual advisor who truly changed my life. Mary Lee saw clients in her tiny, unkempt office in Hollywood or in her beautiful home in Encino in the Valley. She had art everywhere. Letters from and photos of people she had worked with over the years were scattered across her tiny Hollywood office. There were two chairs and an old desk surrounded by boxes and art, so when you walked into her office, you could barely see the floor!

Mary was an older woman, maybe in her mid-to-late seventies, although I never asked her age; it was irrelevant. Her eyes were the most piercing shade of crystal blue, and while her wrinkles showed her age, her face was truly angelic. I do believe she was as close to God as any human being could be.

She often told me stories about how she would visit her husband "on the other side" since he had passed only a few years prior. She described her encounters with him in such detail that I felt as if I had gone there with her. She taught me so much about souls, energy, and our existence beyond the human one. She was the angel I needed in that moment to help me navigate the journey I was about to embark on.

In addition to Kellie and Mary Lee, I had so many amazing women in my corner at that time to help me through this period in my life. Unlike when I was in Chicago, alone and scared, going through that challenging time with Charles, I had a tribe of amazing friends and women in my life. I felt supported, and everyone knew exactly what I was dealing with.

From my perspective, my marriage to Tom was never truly rooted in deep connection or genuine partnership. I realized I had always viewed our relationship from the outside looking in, measuring it by appearances, shared activities, or how I wanted to perceive it, rather than experiencing it from within. We naturally slipped into roles shaped by our individual upbringings, but for me, those roles left me feeling disconnected from myself and from what I truly wanted in a marriage.

I clung to moments that gave the illusion of closeness, whether it was helping with his business, planning dinner parties, or organizing weekend trips with friends, simply to have something to look forward to. Yet beneath it all, the everyday reality we had built together was far from the vision I held for my life.

One day, a friend said something that made me realize our relationship was heading in the wrong direction. Out of respect for our privacy, I will not share details, but that was the moment my inner knowing finally surfaced. That same day, I walked through the door after work and told Tom I wanted us to go to therapy together. At first, he dismissed the idea, saying he did not need therapy. He eventually agreed, but by then much of the damage had already been done. After only a few sessions, I think we both knew what was coming next.

As I've stated before, people come into your life for a reason, a season, or a lifetime. Each relationship and person you encounter, even if just for a few seconds, can change the trajectory of your life forever. Remember the homeless man on the train tracks back in Chicago? Had that incident on the train tracks never occurred, I might never have made that amazing connection with Terri Hemmert and learned as much as I did on those drives to work.

> Can you think of someone like that who was in your life for a short time, but the impact they made stayed with you? Those encounters, I believe, are God or the Universe intervening to teach you something or send you down a different path.

Guided by Grace

As I mentioned in reference to my relationship with Steve, as well as Charles, there are people who come into our lives simply to teach us lessons, and they aren't meant to be in our lives forever. I'm sure you can think of several people who have made a tremendous impact on you, whether positive or negative, but at the end of the day, the lesson was not only valuable but necessary for your growth.

That's intended. As I mentioned in a previous chapter, we can either learn and grow or stay stuck. So, as you look at the relationships that were the most difficult in your life that either didn't last, or are still there trying to teach you something, ask yourself, *What is this person trying to teach me*, or more importantly, *What is the lesson in this?*

This time in my life was filled with great introspection. I went on a true inward journey to really connect with myself and who I wanted to be. I was thirty-three years old, but I felt as if I could see the path toward the end of my life in one direction, and it was filled with anger, alcohol, arguing, and emptiness.

I was at a crossroads. The other path was unknown. It was filled with twists and turns that I could not really see, but I felt a bit of relief when I looked down that path.

The longer I continued to go to therapy, to see Mary Lee, and to do the work on the inside, the further apart Tom and I became. I must admit I still loved him and felt responsible for him and his happiness. (Once again, I was feeling responsible for someone else's feelings above my own.) I didn't want things to go the way they were going, but there was no turning back once I realized that our marriage had been rooted in illusion. I wasn't willing to give up my entire future, knowing that this was going to be the reality, and while there is always the opportunity to work toward reconciliation, I knew deep down that we were on completely different paths. There is no room for reconciliation when you want different things. Once again, just as when I left Chicago and my life Charles behind, I chose to honor myself.

Jennifer Mentesana

I remember walking into my boss's office on Friday morning and telling her I needed to take a few days off. It was a huge risk since I was struggling to perform at work, but I didn't care. I needed space to think, and I couldn't focus at work.

I left work that day and went and sat on the beach in Santa Monica. I must have been quite a sight, sitting on the sand in my business suit, shoes off, and tears pouring down my face. I realized that my marriage was over, but I didn't know what to do. I didn't know what to say to Tom. I was trying to come up with the kindest, most respectful way to tell him I was leaving.

After a couple of hours, I went back to our apartment in Westwood and started packing a suitcase. I wanted to get everything I needed so that I would be packed and ready when Tom got home from work.

I honestly don't remember much about the rest of that evening. It's a blur. I don't remember what I said, or even how he responded. I only remember staring out of the bedroom window on the second story of our walk-up apartment, calling my Grandma Audrey at about midnight. I told her I needed a place to stay for a while. She didn't ask any questions. She simply replied in her thick New Zealand accent, "Well, get your shit and get down here!"

I drove down to Culver City from Westwood (that drive is a complete blur, too), but I remember arriving at my grandma's doorstep with my giant suitcase, tears pouring down my face as I stood in her entryway. She was sitting at the kitchen table with a bottle of Baileys Irish cream and two coffee mugs. The sense of relief I felt being someplace safe, where I knew I could process what was happening and not be judged, was just what I needed.

I know I did not tell Tom that night that I wanted a divorce. I wasn't ready to say those words. But I did know I needed space and time to really be clear on what I wanted. I hoped that after a week or so of space to process what was happening, I would have some perspective and maybe clarity on the situation.

Guided by Grace

Unfortunately, as much as I gained clarity and strength, there was a lot of guilt setting in, and I felt judged for leaving. The emotional roller coaster I was on was unbearable, and most nights after work, I would lie in bed all night long crying and trying to process what was happening.

I look back on that time, and I know I was grieving. It wasn't so much the confusion and fear of getting divorced as it was grieving the loss of my marriage. Although much of our three-year marriage was a struggle, I did care about Tom and didn't want to hurt him. I also knew he wasn't right for me, and I finally accepted that the reasons why we got married were not the foundation of a solid marriage.

We all know that hindsight is 20/20, and I was not as self-aware when we got married as I was after all the inward and spiritual work I had done. However, I still felt a lot of guilt for not only leaving Tom but also for marrying him in the first place, since I had not done the work inside to know what I truly wanted.

Deep down, somewhere in the depths of my soul, I knew he wasn't right for me even before we got married. When he proposed, I got swept up in the moment, and I think both of us did. While I am an extremely spiritual person and believe in marriage as a spiritual union, I also believe that God allows us to make mistakes. We should not compromise our purpose or our authentic path in this lifetime.

I do not believe that human beings should stay married if they are not good for one another. I am confident that my marriage to Tom was intended to teach me something about myself and possibly to teach him about himself, although, again, that is not for me to understand or even explore.

If there is anything I can share with you about getting married, it is this: I hope you understand and love yourself completely before you choose your partner. Do not look for someone else to meet the needs you cannot meet for yourself. A marriage, or any ideal relationship, should complement you, your gifts, your talents, and your purpose. Your connection should elevate your spiritual vibration together.

Ask yourself: Do we make each other better? Do our strengths complement one another? Do we share the same beliefs about faith, family, and core values? The external things can be worked through, but the internal, spiritual connection is what truly matters most. Unless, of course, you want simply a contractual marriage that makes sense on paper.

Through my process of self-development, I realized that not only did I want more than that, I deserved more than that.

I also think, in my case, I am a classic serial problem solver. I have always believed there is nothing I cannot fix or make better. In each of my relationships, I knew deep down that something was not right, but for whatever reason, I chose to hang on, to work harder, or to try to fix it. Remember when I said earlier that everyone has their own path, and you cannot make someone love you or do anything they do not want to do? This is where free will comes into play.

I thought I was strong enough and willing enough to fix all of the issues in my relationships. What I did not realize at the time was that this belief was misguided. It came from a lack of understanding of how divine power truly works. Once I began to do the inner work and learned how energy, self-connection, and a real relationship with God function, I was able to let go of the need to control outcomes. We cannot force anything in this lifetime. Energy, spiritual connection, and love are the only real powers. Those who use fear as power rely on negative energy, and that always backfires. It happens every time.

I had spent several years convincing myself that I could make it work, that we had enough on the outside to make up for what was missing on the inside. I ignored the constant unsettled feeling in my gut, which I still feel now as I write this, remembering what it was like to push down my true feelings and intuition. It was an ache, a longing, and a desire for more that I refused to release out of fear of what might happen. I chose to bury it and tell myself it would go away. I focused on the things I could control, convincing myself that the external aspects of the relationship were what truly mattered.

The major point here is that I ignored the **breadcrumb,** the initial sinking feeling in my gut when we moved to San Diego, and life slowed down enough for me to hear my intuition. And it was not subtle; it was obvious. Even so, I would never take back the experience of being with Tom. We shared many good times and a lot of laughs, and I learned so much about myself and what I wanted in life through that journey. To this day, I am grateful for that period, because I know it was a huge catalyst for where I am now.

Going through difficult times is necessary for growth. Without life-altering challenges, you cannot come out stronger or more prepared for the next phase. Whether in your personal or professional life, mistakes, setbacks, and failures are all part of becoming the best version of you. If it were all "rockets and rainbows" (thank you for that phrase, Mrs. G.), we would never grow into what God intends us to be. That is one of life's greatest keys: it is not about avoiding mistakes or ignoring your intuition, but about choosing to learn from those mistakes and experiences.

Had I not married Tom, I'm not sure I would know what I really wanted out of a marriage, and I certainly wouldn't know what I now know about myself and what I am capable of. The truth is, many people marry and stay married to someone who is not right for them because they are afraid to face the reality of making a different choice. They are afraid of the disappointment of others or the outcome of the situation. But staying in a relationship for the wrong reasons is worse, in my opinion. It's like living a lie and lying to that person every day.

Please understand, I am a big believer and fan of marriage! It is the most incredibly fulfilling and worthwhile relationship if you choose to marry someone who loves you for who you are deep down and not who they expect you to be. But it can be one of the most challenging relationships in your life if you marry the wrong person for reasons that are not rooted in the authenticity of who you are and who you are meant to be. I had finally come to a point through all the inner work I had done that I could no longer ignore my intuition, or God's voice telling me that I was on the wrong path. It was impossible to ignore.

There was no turning back once I connected to my intuition and my spirituality, and as hard and scary as it was to say it out loud, I needed to tell Tom that I wanted a divorce. Before I even got the courage to tell him, Stacy and her husband told me that he had gone back to his hometown. I think he knew that it was over, too. I look back, now that I have perspective, and realize I had been grieving the loss of the marriage for some time, maybe a year, so that by the time the divorce was final, I was no longer attached to the outcome.

Grief, like pain, it's temporary. It's not intended to last unless you choose to stay stuck in it. I look at grief now as a gift. It's a time for processing the pain so that you can come out on the other side stronger, wiser, and ready to take on the next chapter, and that's exactly what I did.

Guided by Grace

Have you ever ignored that quiet voice in your gut, knowing deep down you were making the wrong choice, because you feared the consequences of backing out or convinced yourself you could somehow make it work?

We often do this out of fear of what will happen if we change our minds. We tell ourselves we can fix it, make it work, or push through, but most of the time it cannot work out because, deep down, we know it is not our path.

Once again, I chose to ignore my intuition and push down my instincts out of fear—fear of being alone, fear of failure, and fear of disappointing someone else. Is there a situation you are in right now that you know is not right, but you continue to move forward out of fear of making a change?

Take a moment to journal about that. You do not need to have the answers right now. Simply allow your feelings to surface and put them on paper. The perspective and answers will come more easily once you clear your head and allow your gut to speak.

Chapter 9
The Awakening

"We can no more do without spirituality than we can do without food, shelter, or clothing."
−Ernest Holmes

After Tom left and I was officially moved into my grandma's house (at least until I could get back on my feet), I began to truly take stock of my life. I would come home to my grandma's most nights, exhausted and sad, but relieved that I was moving on with my life and finally had the courage to leave my marriage.

I found myself back at Stacy's many nights when I needed social connection, and she now had a baby boy. I loved to spend time with her and her family, helping with the baby when I could. It gave me hope for a future I would hopefully have, but which still seemed so far away. Most evenings, however, I sat around my Grandma Audrey's kitchen table listening to stories of her life and many from my childhood that I had long forgotten. We talked a lot about my parents' divorce, their marriage, and how it impacted my brothers and me.

Jennifer Mentesana

It was a time of true healing for me. I had already been through a lot at thirty-three years old, and I had very little to be hopeful about. I was broke and again in debt, and my friends were all having babies while I was getting a divorce.

It was a strange time, and I didn't know where to be. I spent a lot of time reading, writing, and getting exercise when I wasn't at work. I had very little passion or purpose at that time, and I remember feeling as though I might end up alone after the past two relationships had failed so miserably.

The bright light in my life was my Grandma Audrey. Thank God for her. She was so wise and had the best perspective on life. For someone who had come from so little and been through so much, she was always grateful and had the most incredible attitude. Except, of course, when you crossed her, which luckily I was smart enough never to do, nor would I ever. I respected her immensely for her authenticity and positive attitude.

I ended up living with my grandma for almost two years, and probably learned more in those two years than I had up until that point. She always had friends stopping by, coming in for coffee or a cup of tea and a chat around the kitchen table. She spent every morning bringing in the neighbor's garbage cans and waving to the kids who played in the alley behind her house. She had a simple life, and it was exactly what I needed to witness at that time.

I realized that she had been alone since Grandpa Walt died, but she was never lonely. My grandpa Walt had passed away a few years earlier, and she had more freedom, community, and joy than she had in years. I was learning that I could create the life I wanted from within, without looking elsewhere and without needing others to fulfill me and create my joy. That revelation was a turning point for me, and I could finally see the forest for the trees.

I had been at KCBS for over a year at this point, and I knew if I didn't close something big soon, I wouldn't be employed for much longer. A

Guided by Grace

few months later, I had an opportunity to bring in a promotional partner to a marketing campaign that one of the marketing sales managers was executing.

It was for a big movie studio release, and the launch event was held at the Playboy Mansion in Hollywood. It was the first project in a long time that I was excited to be a part of, and I had secured a denim line to partner with the release of the film.

All of the Playboy Bunnies were dressed from the waist down in the jeans from the company I was representing. They had no clothes on top but were body-painted from the waist up in the image of *Daredevil*, which was the movie we were promoting. It was pretty creative, and my client (of course, he was a man) loved it! The partnership and event were a huge hit, and little did I know that would be another giant breadcrumb to the path correction I would take next.

Most of the KCBS staff attended the launch event, along with some studio executives and Hollywood socialites. Ben Affleck and Jennifer Garner were a no-show, but the party was so much fun that no one really seemed to notice or care. Prior to this, I had never really socialized with anyone from work. I knew some of the salespeople from chats in the hallway or the occasional sales meeting I participated in, but that was it.

Once the event was underway, and my clients were happy and mingling, I walked up to the main outdoor bar next to the pool (and the infamous grotto) to order a drink. As I was waiting for my drink, I felt this instant rush of energy all over my body as I felt someone brush up against my arm at the bar.

I turned to look, and standing there was a cute sales rep named John. I had spoken to him a few times at work, and he was usually goofing around, making jokes and sarcastic remarks loudly to other salespeople in the office. I honestly hadn't thought much about him before that encounter at the bar.

But there we were, standing next to each other, and it was as if suddenly everyone at the party disappeared, and it was just the two of us standing there alone in our own little world. At that moment, it hit me. I remembered a dream that I had about him just a few nights before! I hadn't remembered it until that moment!

Has that ever happened to you? You see someone or get a phone call from someone after having a dream about them, and you haven't thought of them in forever? It's the strangest, most out-of-body experience. Now, I'm not saying that this was some sort of divine intervention, but I definitely believe it was another giant breadcrumb telling me something was significant about this moment.

What happened next was completely out of character for me, and I don't know what came over me because I hardly knew him, but I blurted out, "I just had a dream about you!" I mean, who says that to someone they hardly know?! But I couldn't stop myself. The words just came out without me thinking or anticipating the outcome. I mean, looking back on it, it sounds pretty cheesy—"I just had a dream about you"—but it was true, and it was such a surreal experience to remember it in that moment. I won't tell you exactly what the dream was about, but let's just say that it was very vivid, and it wasn't G-rated!

John and I ended up talking all night, and a group of us went out in Hollywood after the event. While nothing happened between us, I felt an incredible connection and had a hard time processing how this could happen after working in the same building with him for over a year and hardly ever speaking. I guess my head had been so caught up in my failing marriage and life that I didn't see anything outside of myself.

The next day at work, I arrived earlier than usual, a little excited and nervous to see John and talk to him. When I walked to my desk, I heard him on the phone on the other side of the cubicle, and I got a massive pit in my stomach.

Guided by Grace

After he finished his call, he walked over to my desk and we started talking. I told him that I didn't know what had come over me, and why I decided to tell him I had a dream about him. I was so embarrassed and told him I was sorry since it was inappropriate at a work event, but that's what happens at the Playboy Mansion—it's like Vegas, all your inhibitions go out the window!

He looked at me sincerely, told me it was totally fine, and he was flattered. He held my hand for a moment and then went back to his desk. Over the next few months, we would chat often and discovered we had a lot of mutual friends since he lived in the South Bay (that's where I lived with my girlfriends prior to dating Tom), and we started to build a friendship.

As that year came to an end, so did my employment at KCBS. I started on a journey of entrepreneurship and freelancing through connections I had made over the years in media and marketing.

I worked on a few movie studio release promotions, did some marketing and PR for the denim line I had brought to the Playboy Mansion event, and created some pretty incredible events for the NBA and other entertainment companies.

I was getting back on my feet financially, living at my grandma's, and finding work wherever I could. I took a job at a boutique fashion firm, representing some incredible fashion lines. I dabbled in just about everything, trying to find "my thing."

One project in particular became a pivotal moment for me in discovering my strengths and building confidence in entrepreneurship and event coordination. I was freelancing for an agency responsible for the Lionsgate Films release of *Girl With A Pearl Earring* with Scarlett Johansson and Colin Firth. I worked on the project for several months, executing marketing events and promotions. It was such a fun project, with events in New York and at art galleries in Soho and the Upper East Side, as well as Beverly Hills, ending with a culminating event at Mikimoto Pearls in Beverly Hills.

Jennifer Mentesana

I collaborated with studio executives and promotional partners, coordinated guest lists, catering, and bartenders, and managed marketing for Vermeer Dutch Chocolate Cream Liquor, another partner. At each event, I networked with gallery owners, studio executives, and guests, and discovered I had a natural gift for making connections and building relationships. Traditional sales had always felt focused on closing deals, but this was about building partnerships and making people feel valued. I thrived in this space and loved every minute.

At the Mikimoto event, the GM invited me to a private room and offered to let me wear the most gorgeous strand of Tahitian pearls I had ever seen. I felt like a princess. With the entire cast in attendance, I was incredibly proud of the work I had done. In that moment, I thought I had finally found "my thing" and that this could be the career path I would excel in.

While I didn't go on to build a full career out of that experience, it taught me a valuable lesson: you never know what is around the corner. As the saying goes, when God closes a door, He opens a window. The key is to walk through what is open if it feels right and to trust that the path, even if it looks like a detour, may lead to something greater.

The **breadcrumb** I uncovered was my gift for connecting with people, building relationships, and serving those relationships for the greater good. That gift has stayed with me ever since, and it has served me in more ways than I can count.

John and I stayed in touch during that period, mainly talking over the phone and sharing stories about our lives, failed marriages, and just about everything else. He had a five-year-old daughter, and his entire life was about her. He told me stories about their weekend activities and funny things she would say. While it was hard to keep our connection at a distance, mostly through phone conversations, I loved every moment of that time we had getting to know one another. I hadn't experienced that level of connection with someone in a very long time, and I cherished it.

Guided by Grace

There are periods in our lives that are not meant for exponential growth but for healing. Time for taking a pause to check in and evaluate where we are, who we are, and where we want to go. Usually, this comes after trauma or pain. While it's difficult to go through it, it is a necessary stage of evaluation before you can move forward again and get back on track. If you choose to ignore this period and throw yourself into distractions to not process what you have been through, you are dismissing the lesson that was intended from the pain or trauma you went through.

After my relationship with Charles and the internal trauma I experienced from all that had happened between us, I dove into another relationship without really processing what had happened. I didn't want to feel it. I wanted to move on without truly understanding what had happened and how to avoid making the same decisions that were not rooted in my purpose or my path.

My failed marriage to Tom was almost entirely a result of not processing my previous relationship and the desire not to listen to my intuition. I chose to ignore all the signs that told me he was wrong for me because I didn't want to feel the pain of what had happened with Charles. I didn't allow myself to heal, and I chose to throw myself into a relationship that was a house of cards.

Here's the toughest part. Sometimes, even when we think we are done grieving, God has other plans. Have you ever noticed yourself trying to rush through something to get to the next phase, only to have something keep holding you back? Usually, that something is God telling you it's not time yet.

I've had to learn this lesson too many times in my lifetime, and often still do. I admit I am not the most patient person, as once I see something clearly, I'm ready to move forward, but that's not always how it works.

The answers come in God's time. If we can slow down and trust the process, continuing to do the work to move through the pain or lessons, the *right path* will reveal itself. However, if we force things against the natural progression of the Universe, those outcomes are usually not favorable. It's like God is up there watching you and saying, "Oh boy, here she goes again. This is yet another lesson she's going to have to learn the hard way because she's being impatient." Which is fine! Life is all about the delicate balance of learning lessons so we can become who we are meant to be and following the breadcrumbs down the path that leads us to our true life's purpose.

While much of the next few years after my divorce were lonely, extremely challenging, and uncomfortable, they were absolutely necessary to the transformation I needed to make within myself.

Up until that point in my life, I was looking at everything from an outward perspective. I worked toward accumulating jobs, money, relationships, and security. And in the end, none of it had worked. I was emotionally and financially depleted, with no real career to speak of and no home of my own.

However, this reality was exactly what I needed to choose an entirely new way of living and a new path for myself. Course correction was what I needed, and it was imperative that I take the time to process where I was and where I was headed if I was going to go down a new path.

Once again, I was at a crossroads, and I needed to *feel* the emotional and mental pain of where I was at that stage in my life instead of continuously pushing it down and jumping into another job, relationship, or decision that was not rooted in what I truly wanted for my life. I no longer worried about what others thought (except, of course, Grandma Audrey, and she was always proud of me), including my parents, friends, and colleagues.

I wanted to feel what was right for me, instead of thinking about it from an outside perspective and based on what I had been taught or what others expected of me. That is what our society does. We have norms and expectations of what it looks like to be a responsible adult. A young woman in her early thirties *should* be either married and having babies or on a career path to success. I was doing neither of those things. It took me facing that reality to see how far gone from my path I had gotten.

I continued to flounder and try to find a job that would pay me a decent salary, provide benefits, and have growth potential while I did some much-needed soul searching. I got hired yet again at another media company, still not following the breadcrumbs toward my purpose, but continuing to search for financial stability. It was a stable, structured job, and I looked forward to having some routine in my life again. I threw myself into this new role, hoping to find some real success again. Although this time I was fully aware that this was not my path to my true purpose, I knew I needed it to boost my confidence and be able to provide for myself.

I was still paying off debt from my marriage on top of my own credit card bills, car payment, and paying for what little groceries I could afford for myself and my grandma. I cooked her dinner on occasion when I got home early enough to eat. Most days at that new job, I was in the office until after 7 p.m. and drove home exhausted, then went right to bed.

John and I continued to talk and began spending more time together. He came to visit me one day at my grandma's house. I will admit, I felt a little embarrassed to be in my mid-thirties and living with my grandma. All of our baggage was out in the open for each other to see. There was no hiding the past, no creating a perfect picture, no fantasy or illusion.

My grandma Audrey adored John. She loved his New Jersey accent, his confident attitude, and his Italian upbringing. She had always been a sucker for Italian men. He would even stop by to sit with her at the kitchen table when I was not home. They built a special bond, and I know my grandma appreciated the attention. Most of her visitors in those days were older ladies from the neighbourhood, or me, so John's company was something she truly cherished.

Jennifer Mentesana

One of my stipulations for John and me to spend more time together and start officially dating was that he needed to meet with Mary Lee once a week to make sure he was in a place of authenticity and on a path to spiritual awareness.

Since he was going through a divorce, and I had as well, we were in an extremely vulnerable place. I wanted any relationship we might have to be built on a solid foundation, based on real connection and truth, and not on being a Band-Aid for each other.

We were very conscious of this and spent a lot of time talking about what we wanted and what we didn't want. It was the most mature and genuine relationship I've ever had with a man. Our relationship was built from a place of love, respect, and spirituality, which I am forever grateful for.

Most of my friends initially did not approve of my relationship with John, and understandably so. They were skeptical about the fact that he was not yet officially divorced when we met and had a daughter. Aside from the obvious reasons for being skeptical, I believe they saw our relationship as a conflict to their beliefs about marriage and way of life. I understand to this day how they felt, and respected their feelings, but I knew better about what the potential of our connection could be, not only for us, but for his daughter.

My grandma and Mary Lee were my primary sources of support at that time, and although my mom didn't say much about my relationship (and frankly I didn't really talk to her about John much at that time), I know she was worried about me, my choices in men so far, and the fact that he was divorcing with a daughter. It's natural for those who love us and want the best for us to be concerned about our choices, and what they see the situation to be. But I trusted my intuition and my connection with God when it came to my relationship with John. That was the only approval I needed.

I decided to stay faithful and connected to the relationship I was building with God, and trusting my grandma and Mary Lee, who saw me for who I truly was, and not what anyone else wanted me to be. I knew that they both had more wisdom from a lifetime of experiences than anyone else I knew.

Friendships are some of the most precious gifts in life. They can be the most incredible sources of support, but often, if you live your life in a way that does not reflect the values of your friends, this may cause turmoil in your relationships. Not everyone shares the same values, and often, your values can change over time depending on the season you are in.

My friends were in *very* different places in their lives at that time. I was going through a divorce, reconfiguring the path of my life, and most of them were recently married, having babies, and settling down.

> If you have never done a values exercise, I highly recommend visiting my website (listed at the back of this book) to download one. There are many versions available, but for ease of access, you can find the exercise directly on my site.
>
> Unlike typical values exercises, the one I provide blends your core values with your natural gifts, talents, and passions. The result is a powerful and personalized roadmap that helps you move toward a path that truly aligns with who you are.

Determining your core values, in addition to following the breadcrumbs from the Universe, will guide you through your decisions as you make the most challenging ones of your life. If you make each decision from your top five core values, you can never go wrong because you are making them from a place of who you innately are and what is most important to you.

Keep in mind that over time, as you grow, evolve, and experience life, your core values may change a bit, especially if you decide to have a family. Your kids and their well-being will likely become one of your top values; others may still be important to you, but no longer among your top five.

For me, at that time, my top five values were Love, Authenticity (which is still one of my top five), Freedom, Community, and Faith. I knew as long as I continued to meet with Mary Lee, staying grounded in my faith and connection, the right path would unfold for me. I chose not to be influenced by anyone or anything else around me.

I was safe living with my grandmother, had a steady job and income, and hoped that the rest would figure itself out. With John seeing Mary Lee and doing the work to understand himself from a spiritual and enlightened perspective, I trusted that the right path would unfold for us.

Once John and I were officially dating, I had another incredible dream. I dreamt that I was back in high school at a party with all of my friends. We were sitting on a couch in someone's living room, and I was next to Steve (yes, the same Steve I had dated off and on since the sixth grade). In the dream, Steve and I were together. Then I looked over at the coffee table and saw my cell phone ringing, which was strange since there were no cell phones when I was in high school. The caller ID showed it was John. Steve picked up the phone, looked at it, smiled, and then handed it to me.

When I told Mary Lee about the dream, she said she was not surprised. She explained that it was a sign that I could let the past go and trust that John was the one for me. From that moment, I never looked back.

John also coached me through many work challenges. Having been in the business for years, he helped me navigate office politics. My boss at the time (let's call her "Sandra") worked out of the New York office, and I was glad she was not nearby because she was an intimidating woman. You could feel her energy coming through the phone and she would often yell at and berate the salespeople during our meetings. This was

Guided by Grace

before Zoom, so we were always on large conference calls with sales reps from across the country.

I was the newest on the team, and I did my best to keep my head down and focus on closing business. It was again a very toxic environment, but thankfully, the LA office I worked out of had some amazing people. I connected with many of them, and it made my job more enjoyable.

On one occasion, Sandra came out to LA with her assistant, with whom I had become friends. After our meetings for the day, Sandra invited me to go with her and her assistant to a spa and stay overnight at her vacation property nearby. It sounded like a great opportunity, and I was excited to get some time with her so she could get to know me, and hopefully, we would create a positive relationship. We went to a fabulous spa, sat by the pool, and relaxed for the afternoon. She treated us to the entire experience, and it was an incredible day.

We left the spa and drove to her home on a private beach just north, and settled right on the sand. You could hear the waves crashing up on the deck. It was spectacular. The next day, Sandra told me she was leaving to go to an appointment, and I could stay the afternoon and work from there. I was grateful and took the opportunity to work out on the patio with my laptop since it was a gorgeous spring day.

When she returned a few hours later, I was still out on the patio working, and one of the women who lived there full-time had come out to strike up a conversation with me. When Sandra saw us talking outside on the deck, she went nuclear on me. The rage coming out of her was earth-shattering. I mean, never in my entire life had I encountered anyone who spoke to me that way... not even my dad or my previous boss from Q101 in Chicago. (Are we noticing a pattern here?)

I was stunned. I just sat there, taking it, tears pouring down my face. She berated me for not really working and taking advantage of her generosity. The woman who lived there that I was speaking with was so embarrassed, she just got up and went inside.

Jennifer Mentesana

After Sandra was done completely annihilating me, she went inside and got on a call. I walked into the house, grabbed my things, and ran out to my car. I was sobbing, frozen at the car door, not sure what to do. I called John, crying so hard he could barely hear me. Sandra's assistant, my friend Caroline, ran out to the car and begged me not to leave. She told me it would be so much worse if I left. I would never be able to gain Sandra's respect, and she would likely find a way to fire me.

Can you believe that? Imagine that happening to an employee in today's corporate environment. Although deep down I knew what she did was wrong on so many levels, including bringing me to her private residence in the first place, I swallowed my tears and my pride and went back into the house.

She didn't apologize, but she told me she realized that how she spoke to me had "stunned" me (those were the exact words she used). It was as if she were criticizing me for the way I reacted. I didn't say anything; I just listened, and after that she never said another word about it.

I faked my emotions the rest of the evening, smiling, nodding, and trying to enjoy myself through dinner, but I was suffering inside. The next morning, at the crack of dawn, I woke up and drove home before anyone was up.

About a month later, I called Caroline and told her I wanted to report Sandra. I knew what she had done was wrong, and I was so uncomfortable every time I spoke to her after that.. I couldn't shake the feeling that she had this control over me. Caroline begged me not to. So instead, I quit.

Guided by Grace

> You will encounter people in your life for all different reasons. As we have discussed in previous chapters, they are usually there to teach you something. How can you look at a past relationship in your life that was difficult or downright awful as a gift? If you feel compelled to do so, take a moment to journal about that relationship to shift your perspective to seeing the gift in the challenge.

Going back to the analogy I used about seeing those people as guardian angels wearing masks, if they took off their masks, they would be actual angels in disguise. I believe those people are there for significant lessons. Dramatic experiences that you chose to have even before you were born to help you become who you were meant to be, or to learn that lesson so that you can teach others.

In this particular case with Sandra, it's hard for me to say that she was a guardian angel, but she was definitely someone I pulled in to teach me a lesson I had previously ignored. Have you noticed that in your life? If you continue to ignore a pattern that repeats itself, the pattern gets louder and more difficult to ignore.

For whatever reason, I continued to attract people into my life who were mentally, emotionally, and verbally abusive, much like the dynamic with my father. It is very common to draw on experiences and people that mirror what you have lived through in the past, giving you the chance to learn a lesson. If you continue to ignore those lessons or hold onto unhealthy habits, you will repeat them over and over until they become so obvious that they take over your life. It is like the definition of insanity: doing the same thing repeatedly while expecting a different result.

In that instance, the lesson for me was to stand up for myself, tell Sandra it was not acceptable to speak to me that way, pack up my things, walk away, and then report her to HR. Fear kept me from doing that.

This is common in romantic relationships as well. You continue to pick the same type of guy because, for whatever reason, you are subconsciously attracted to the way they treat you. You can break this pattern by looking inward and asking yourself why you continue to attract people who treat you that way.

Ask yourself: *Where is that coming from?* Usually, it is because, somewhere deep inside, the part of you that was hurt when you were young believes you deserve to be treated that way. An experience from your past created the belief that this behavior is normal. Because you expect it, you continue to draw those people and situations into your life until you learn the lesson and change the pattern.

Psychologists will often say it comes down to low self-esteem or a lack of self-respect. I believe that can be true, but I also believe those dynamics are formed when you are young, shaped by the people around you who are supposed to love you. For their own reasons, often rooted in their own low self-esteem or lack of self-respect, they project those struggles onto you. In my case, I believe the dynamic with my father, and his inability to be emotionally available to me, created patterns in my relationships not only with men but also with people in positions of authority.

Remember, you come into this world pure and perfect, created in the likeness of God and His love for you. What happens after you are born, influenced by the people and environments that shape you, forms the perspective you develop about yourself and the world. Over time, you begin to forget who you were born to be, and the perspectives, actions, and experiences of others, along with societal expectations, shape your new reality.

To change your perception of yourself, let that really sink in. It's not your fault. You weren't born to be critical, insecure, or to lack self-esteem; those beliefs came from the messages you were given by the people around you. By the way, it's not their fault either. Our parents, and those around us, including most of society, lacked the awareness and tools to manage their perceptions of the world. They are a product of their environment, and so on, and so on.

That is why it is incredibly important for you to do this internal work on yourself so that you can see who you truly are, and who you were born to be, and remove the perceptions of the world that were projected onto you. This is especially important if you are raising children or planning to raise children. Be aware of your own perceptions of the world, society, your beliefs, and how you project them on your children and the world!

Imagine how incredible humanity could be if we all did this work! If we all cared enough to take the time to see the truth about our human race and how flawed our perceptions have been. It is not our job to control society and others. We are only responsible for our own beliefs, actions, and perceptions of the world and our part in it. God sees every human being for who they truly are, and all he wants is for us to actualize that version of ourselves so we can create a better human race!

I see a future without war, government control, or diminished society. I see a world where the entire human race is enlightened, using their unique gifts and talents to create a better existence for all. Wouldn't that be amazing?!

Imagine a life where you can have whatever you want, but don't *need* anything because you are truly fulfilled in your existence. You are living the life you want, with the people you love most, who lift you up, and you lift them up to be the highest actualization of themselves. Envision a world where human beings are in the form of beautiful souls, walking around on Earth, living pure lives.

That is actually possible, but it takes the entire human race to see the truth. How will you be a part of that possibility? What will you start doing today to become that version of yourself and hold yourself to that standard so that others can see you and want to do the same?

Can you think of a relationship in your life right now that may not be healthy, and that is potentially a pattern for you? Look very closely at these relationships and what they are trying to tell you or teach you. Have you experienced the same unhealthy dynamic before?

We only pull in things that we need to help us grow, evolve, and learn. Every important relationship in your life that has any sort of meaning was designed for a specific reason. I'm not talking about casual acquaintances who don't have much bearing on your life. I'm talking about the closer, more impactful ones that are very positive and uplifting, or the ones that caused trauma that forced you to learn about yourself.

Those are the relationships you need to look at closely. Again, ask yourself, *What is this relationship trying to teach me about myself? How can I look at this relationship as a gift for becoming a better version of myself?* It could be a boss, a friend, a coworker, or even a significant other. Notice if there is a pattern to the dynamic you have with this person. If so, that's a key indicator of a lesson you intend to learn but haven't quite gotten the memo yet.

> Take a few moments to journal about relationships in your life, past or present, that were unhealthy. See if you can notice a pattern of repeating the same types of relationships over and over again.
>
> Do you choose friends or partners who disrespect you or treat you poorly? Ask yourself if there is a reason you continue to invite relationships with the same unhealthy dynamic. How can you view those patterns as an opportunity to look inward and examine your role in drawing those people into your life?

Guided by Grace

I had a pattern of finding abusive people of authority and allowing them to impact my experiences, and often my perception of myself, just as my father had many years before. He impacted my entire childhood and how I felt about myself.

I needed to learn that I was strong and deserved to be treated with respect and kindness and to be shown unconditional love. I never did anything to deserve to be treated that way, but somehow, those experiences left me feeling horrible about myself, beaten down, and made to feel less than or somehow inadequate.

I had many people in my life who tried to make me feel that way, and often they were successful. But the truth was that I allowed their behavior to impact me because it was what I expected for myself. This was what I subconsciously told myself was "normal" because it was what I grew up with. I needed to become stronger than their power over me so that I could become the woman I am today.

When that incident happened with Sandra, I felt powerless. She was my direct boss, and there was no one present I could go to whom I felt safe with other than Caroline. Caroline was a confidante and a friend and someone I could lean on, but she was not in a position to help me when it came to my situation. I knew I could go to HR, but I was relatively new to the company, and Sandra was a highly respected and powerful executive. I didn't see that as an option at the time.

It was still a time in corporate America when the attitude was that if you complained or went to HR, you were considered weak and a traitor. You would get a bad reputation in the industry, and it would stay with you throughout your career.

If that incident happened today (and I had the courage to report her), especially in the state of California, that company would face a lawsuit. That incident with Sandra would have definitely been considered harassment, but back then, the lines weren't so clearly defined. In fact, I'm pretty sure her inviting me to her house to stay overnight with her and four other women who may or may not have been gay was completely inappropriate. I did feel somewhat held captive, even though she never said I *had* to stay. There was an indication that I couldn't say no, and if I had left after she went nuclear on me, I felt my job was on the line. I felt violated and afraid.

Incidents like that are what helped shape some of the laws we have today that protect employees from employers like Sandra, who have too much power and don't know how to manage people other than with control and fear.

I am so grateful that today we have more guardrails around the amount of power and control executives can exert over employees, and that there is actually a shift in the culture of management. Amazing leaders and consultants like Jon Gordon, who teach the power of positivity, treating each other with respect and dignity, and focusing on positive energy leadership for executive teams and organizations, are making huge shifts in our culture.

For me, this incident, although I didn't necessarily handle it as confidently as I could have, was the final straw in my journey to taking my power back in my career.. I no longer questioned what I had done to deserve this treatment and instead realized that this was someone who was weak and was taking her own issues and frustrations out on me. I actually had nothing to do with that incident; I just happened to be the right person, at the right time, in the wrong place.

Once I saw that, it shifted how I viewed myself. Up until that point, I believed that there was a certain amount of abuse I was expected to endure if I wanted to be respected and successful in this business.

I also learned, over the years in that industry, that women are threatened by other women in business and rarely treat each other with respect and empowerment. They are highly competitive, and instead of building each other up, they look for ways to tear each other down. This is, of course, also the case outside of corporate America. There

Guided by Grace

have been so few women at the top levels of leadership that the belief was that there simply was not enough room for all of us.

If you've ever had a corporate job, have you noticed that most of the powerful women had to be extremely tough, ruthless, and almost angry to get to the top? Very few of them were viewed as feminine (although Val Maki is one of the great female leaders in media sales who led herself with class, dignity, and strength while still exuding femininity and grace). I'm not saying that all women need to be feminine, or that they should be in any way soft and docile. What I am saying is that there has been a culture in our country that if you are a woman and you want to be successful, you have to be tougher and more cunning than any man around you.

I believe that philosophy is changing, but I can't speak to it as definitively now as I've been out of the corporate world since 2009. Many of the women I know in my community who are in corporate jobs say it's different, and it seems to have evolved a great deal.

The true God-given and innate power of women is to possess incredible intuition and see each other for their strengths, authenticity, and desire to make the world and people around them better. That is how we can lift each other up and be more successful together! If we tear each other down with our insecurities, that helps no one. That is the way of the unenlightened, uninspired, in-it-for-themselves leaders of the past.

I look back on my career often and think about how if only one of my managers had taken the time to really see me for who I am, my gifts and strengths, and how they could nurture those gifts to become great, how successful I could have become in that business (I actually think Michael Damsky, at WXRT in Chicago, my first boss in radio, would have managed me that way but I didn't stick around long enough to find out.)

In those days, that kind of thinking was scarce, if present at all. You had to be tough and fit into a box that was identified long before you got hired. Truthfully, people didn't have the tools and resources to be enlightened enough to operate that way. In the end, that career wasn't the path I was intended to follow long-term. I was only on that path to learn so that I could become who God intended me to be and to learn the lessons along the way that would ultimately become my purpose. I was designed for something much greater than I could have ever imagined. I just didn't know it yet.

> Take a few minutes to reflect on how your relationships, whether personal or professional, have shaped you over time, either positively or negatively. Every lesson can be viewed as a blessing that contributes to who you are becoming. It is up to you to decide how you see your past, present, and future. Every challenge, relationship, and experience can serve as a step toward your purpose if you choose to see it that way.

Chapter 10
A New Beginning

"We must be willing to get rid of the life we've planned, so as to have the life that is waiting for us. The old skin has to be shed before the new one can come."
–Joseph Campbell

Fortunately, Traci, one of the managers I had collaborated with on a project a few months before I quit, left the company and was hired at Google. Google was on a massive hiring spree, specifically looking for radio salespeople to build out its new automated radio platform.

Traci recommended me to the top recruiting manager for an interview. It was exciting to interview with Google in those days. It was early 2006, and the tech boom was in full swing. Google (now Alphabet) was (and still is) one of the most powerful technology companies in the world.

I had zero experience in tech, but the momentum in media was shifting in that direction, and it was an incredible opportunity for old-school radio people like me to interview with a company like Google.

Jennifer Mentesana

I went through eight interviews in all. It was a grueling but respectful process. The vibe (I interviewed at the Irvine campus) was fun and relaxed. There were ping-pong tables, pool tables, lounge areas, healthy snacks, and opportunities to "play at work" everywhere.

This was a whole new environment for me, such a drastic change from the corporate offices and energy I was surrounded by for most of my career. They had full-blown restaurants inside the building (designed to keep employees on campus during the workday); everything was thought out to keep employees happy, engaged, and at work for the entire day, and even into the evening. Meals were included (breakfast, lunch, and dinner), so there was no reason to rush home or leave early to eat.

It was a young person's dream environment. I remember feeling a little detached during the interview process, like I didn't really fit in, but I was so in awe of the prospect of being considered to work for Google that it didn't matter. At that point, I had lost all concept of what the "right place" was for me, and I had so many different experiences in the media culture that I was learning to navigate just about anything.

After the three-month interview process, it finally came down to the final decision. Every employee at that time needed to provide their college transcripts with a high GPA to be hired (I don't remember the exact number but I think it was a 4.0).

Needless to say, I did not have a high GPA in college; I was always pretty much an average student except in the classes I was passionate about. I remember sitting in the parking lot after my last interview, praying. For the first time in my life, I prayed for God to let happen what was meant to happen. I didn't pray for the job or anything tangible. I just trusted that whatever would happen was the right path for me. Mary Lee really made an impact on my spiritual awareness and relationship with God, and I felt safe trusting Him to know what outcome was best.

When I got the phone call that I didn't get the job, I wasn't sad, scared, or disappointed. I trusted that Google was not my path, and for the first

Guided by Grace

time in my adult life, I felt at peace about where I was professionally and personally.

My relationship with John was going well, and while I was still living with my grandma, I was in a much better place than I had been in recent years. I was finding myself again, knowing who I was and what I deserved, and most importantly, I had God by my side.

Ironically, not even two weeks later, I got a call from the same recruiter who had brought me into Google for an interview. He was now recruiting for another tech company, and they too, were hiring experienced radio salespeople for their automation platform.

He told me that I did so well in the interview process with Google that I should interview at this new startup called Spot Runner. It was a technology-based ad agency and had only been in operation for a few years.

I moved quickly through the interview process and was hired onto the national sales team, responsible for securing national advertisers for the company. It was a blast. The environment was fun and energetic, and the people I worked with were completely different from those in my past experiences. There was only one other woman on our team of five, and she and I got along great without any drama or competition. All of the managers I reported to were men.

For the most part, working for men was not an issue for me. Aside from my boss at Q101, I had always found it easier to work with men. I never played into competition with women, because I simply did not care enough about that dynamic. With men, I could be myself and focus on my work and talents. As long as there was no unhealthy dynamic, such as a controlling egomaniac or a boss trying to hit on me, I was fine.

The managers at Spot Runner were the most influential and positive relationships I'd had in my career since WXRT. They were from the Silicon Valley tech environment, so there wasn't the same old boys' club mentality going on.

Jennifer Mentesana

I had success quickly, as a lot of the national advertisers were curious and inspired by the new technology emerging in media. I was able to close pretty big campaigns with Buy.com (a competitor of Amazon at the time), NBC's *Deal or No Deal* with Howie Mandel, and Creditreport.com, which became one of my biggest accounts. The national sales team at that point was focused on building relationships with larger clients and educating them on the benefits of our company. I was great at this, and much like my role during the movie studio release projects, I knew how to cultivate relationships and create partnerships. I had finally found my niche in sales. Life was good, I was doing well at work, and my relationship with John was accelerating.

John and I had some ups and downs during that period. He had a hard time managing the challenges that came with divorce with a child, including massive guilt, and he often retreated and removed himself emotionally. For the most part, I managed that all relatively well. There was a time when I was almost living with him after he bought a new home, and we really started to settle into our relationship. I realized that I would need to take a step back myself if this was going to work. I didn't want to make the same mistakes I had in my previous relationships, and I wanted to allow things to unfold naturally. He hadn't quite dealt with all of the emotions that come along with divorcing with a child involved, and he needed space and time to do that.

It was incredibly hard for me, but I left one day with most of my things and didn't come back for a few months. It was the perspective and time he needed to see what he truly wanted, and time for him to be with his daughter alone, and to see what was best for her.

When I started spending more time there again, his daughter, Olivia, asked me one day, "Where did you go? I thought you weren't coming back, and I was sad!" I didn't realize the impact I had already begun to make on her life, and I'm so glad John and I took the time to really work through everything before we made our relationship more permanent.

I finally felt like I was ready to move out of Grandma Audrey's and get a place of my own. When John asked me to move in with him, I was

Guided by Grace

ecstatic. I figured this was the most important next step in our relationship, to see if we could actually live together, share a home, and a life with each other and Olivia. Her time was split exactly 50/50 between her parents' homes.

She lived half of the time with her mom, Julie, in the home she had been raised in, and the other half of the time she was with us. We lived only a mile or so away from her mom's, so the back and forth was logistically pretty easy. She spent Monday, Wednesday, and Friday evenings with us, and every other Saturday. I loved our time together when she was with us. I absolutely adored her, and I know she was fond of me from the very beginning.

I never tried to act like her mom or even act like a parent. I was an adult who loved her and wanted only the best for her, like an auntie. The three of us had so much fun together. On weekends, we would go to the beach or barbecue with friends, and during the week, it became common for me to pick her up from school when John couldn't get there in time. She was my little buddy, and we were creating a special bond.

I remember only one time when she tried to test me. She and I were home alone, and Julie left instructions for John to make sure she got her Kumon math homework done. When I told Olivia she needed to get started, she told me she didn't need to do it and that she could skip one day.

When I tried to convince her she needed to start, she got upset and told me no. I called John, and he didn't pick up, so I called her mom. I had never spoken to Julie before, but I knew if I didn't get her involved, it was going to be an issue.

When I called Julie and told her Olivia told me she didn't need to do her homework, she said, "Oh, she absolutely does, please put her on the phone!" She told Olivia to knock it off and to listen to whatever I told her to do. And then she told Olivia that if she ever did that again, she would be in huge trouble. Julie then asked to speak to me and told me she was grateful that I had called her and said that if Olivia ever did that again, to let her know. I realized at that moment, the very first time I ever spoke with Julie, that we would have a very respectful and considerate relationship going forward.

As time went on, we were pretty settled in our lives. John was doing well as a sales manager at a big radio station in Los Angeles, and I was thriving at Spot Runner. Life was finally back on track, and for the first time in a long time, I could enjoy things without worrying about money, my job, or my relationship. What a concept! I remember thinking that I wanted to pinch myself. My debt from my marriage was nearly paid off after years of struggling, and I was truly happy, this time on the inside as well as the outside.

When John proposed on a warm September evening in front of a full moon on the Manhattan Beach pier, I was so incredibly happy! It was so different than the first time. I was relaxed and completely in the moment. There was no pomp and circumstance, just John and me, and a guy who had pulled up on his bike with a boom box blaring the song "Don't Stop Believin'" by Journey.

It was as if the Universe, or God, sent that guy to the pier that evening just to play that song for us. I will never forget it. All that I had been through since my parents' divorce, college, and the rollercoaster of a career and relationships that had failed led to this moment, and I knew I was exactly where I was meant to be, with the person I was meant to be with.

Here's the thing about life: God wants you to be happy. He wants you to live fully with all of the love, joy, happiness, purpose, and success you possibly can. But He also has a plan for your life, and it isn't always what you think. So, when you try to control it, or live out of alignment with what your soul and God's purpose for you is, it's going to be difficult.

Things will continue to show up to challenge you and make your life harder, to show you the path forward. Often, you will have to go

Guided by Grace

through major challenges and excruciating pain to come out on the other side stronger, toward the path you are meant to live. With each challenge comes opportunity, and it is up to you to see the opportunity in the challenge, to move through the pain, and not resist it. The pain leads to your purpose, so if you ignore it, push it down, or put a Band-Aid on it, it will return.

Here's the most challenging thing about relationships. It's often hard to know if someone is right for you when you fall in love. Sometimes you aren't even in love so much as you are in love with the idea of being in love.

It is also possible that many of your insecurities are masked through these relationships because you pull in energy that you recognize. It's not really the person, or their soul, that you see; it's what that person represents for whatever reason you need in your life at that time.

There is a reason fifty percent of marriages don't last. Marriage is an incredible partnership. It can be the most beautiful relationship of your lifetime. I do believe in soulmates, that we actually travel through lifetimes with certain souls that continue to be in our lives as different people. I have a few of them. Some are friends, and one is my husband. When you meet a soulmate, you just know. The connection is so powerful that a locomotive cannot keep you apart.

But often, life, circumstances, and our own lessons keep us from either marrying our soulmates or staying together. Remember in previous chapters where I talked about how people come into your life for a reason, a season, or a lifetime? If you haven't done the work to remove the blocks and the limiting beliefs that hold you back in your life, not only will you not recognize your soulmate, but you won't be ready to share life with them.

If I hadn't gone through all that I did in my previous relationships, I would never have even noticed John, much less connected and fallen in love with him. I was so open and ready to receive real love that when it arrived, it hit me so hard it was impossible to ignore.

Jennifer Mentesana

If you have not done the work, removed all the layers of pain, and pushed down the stuff you have chosen not to deal with, you will not be in a position to receive real, depth-of-your-soul, earth-shattering love.

If I hadn't found Mary Lee and hadn't gone inward to truly connect with myself and build a relationship with God first, I don't believe I would have ever been able to truly see John. My previous adult romantic relationships were mostly shaped by external influences: the noise in my head, societal expectations, and the opinions of others. I was making choices based on what looked good on the outside, rather than what felt right in my heart and, more importantly, in my soul.

If any of this resonates with you, and you're in a relationship where you feel a disconnect, I'm not telling you to walk away. What I am encouraging is a deeper inquiry. If you desire a truly fulfilling life, one that aligns with the core of who you are, then having a partner who sees and honors that version of you is essential.

If you're currently single and longing to meet someone who will truly see you, I encourage you to begin by reconnecting with your essence, your relationship with yourself, and your higher power. That inner work is the foundation for everything else.

Not only will it open you up to who you truly are, it will attract the right person, most aligned with your soul. I should also add that if you want to create a deeper connection with the person you are with, it's entirely possible. It requires deep commitment from both parties and dedication to doing the work to get to a level of connection (through God or your higher power) that is so deep, nothing can stand in the way of your relationship. If that is what you are looking for, trust me, it is possible! And it is so worth the effort!

John proposed in late September, and we were married on December 1st of that same year! Since both of us had been married before and this was not our first rodeo, John and I were more committed to our relationship and to being married than to having a wedding and all the pomp and circumstance that comes along with that. We had been there, and done that, and neither of us needed that again.

Having said that, we did have a beautiful, small ceremony on the sand in Manhattan Beach. It was a beautiful but very cold and windy winter day. (To this day, our family and friends remind us how cold it was!) John, Olivia, and I stood in the center of a heart drawn in the sand, with rose petals outlining it. Our closest friends and family surrounded us around the heart, and we exchanged vows with my uncle as the officiator. We had an intimate reception at our home in Manhattan Beach with incredible food, friends, and music, and we danced the night away. It was perfect.

> Pause for a moment and reflect on where you are in your journey of love. If you are in a relationship, what would it feel like to experience complete peace and alignment with your partner? To know, deep in your soul, that you are with the person meant for you? If you are not currently in a relationship, what would it look like to prepare your heart and life to welcome that kind of love?
>
> The truth is, finding your soulmate begins with you. It's about showing up as the most authentic version of yourself, the person God created you to be. When you live in your true essence, without masks, pretenses, or roles you think you "should" play, you naturally draw in the kind of love that reflects who you truly are.
>
> So ask yourself: *Who do I want to be in a relationship with? What energy do I want to give and receive?* When you align with that vision and do the inner work to become it, you create an atmosphere where the right person can recognize and be drawn to your light. This is the heart of attracting your soulmate: being open, genuine, and rooted in your true identity.

Chapter 11
Letting Go of Control

Sometimes letting things go is an act of far greater power than defending or hanging on."
−Eckhart Tolle

As John, Olivia, and I settled into our new lives as a family, a profound sense of peace settled into my soul. I knew this was the person I was meant to be with, and all the heart-wrenching challenges and relationships I had endured over the past twenty years had paved the way for this one. Never had I felt so completely settled in with who I was, free from fear and doubt, and the need for constant distraction from reality had disappeared. I was content.

Every night after work, we would cook together, spend time talking about our future, or spend time with Olivia and her schoolwork, sports, and activities. Life was fantastic. I was working hard in my role as an account manager at Spot Runner and was finally feeling like life was in the flow.

Jennifer Mentesana

It wasn't long before John and I started talking about having a baby. For me, that was always part of my plan, but I had spent so much time over the years focusing on my financial stability, relationships, and getting to a place where I could finally be ready to bring a child into the world.

There is never a perfect time to have a baby, as most parents will tell you. There will always be a little bit of fear and the question: *Am I really ready to be a parent?* But I can honestly say that at almost thirty-six years old, I was one hundred percent ready, and it was definitely time to start trying since I knew I was closing in on the end of my reproductive years.

Within about six months of trying to get pregnant, my doctor recommended I do some tests to ensure my hormones and everything were in working order, since I was on the older side. After a few tests, he put me on Clomid (a horrible fertility medication that makes your hormones wacky by increasing your estrogen levels to produce more eggs), and nothing happened.

After a full year of trying, we decided to investigate further what may be going on. Come to find out, after that first year, there was nothing wrong with my egg production, and I didn't need the medication my doctor had put me on that made me moody, horribly depressed (please make sure your doctor doesn't put you on any medication before you truly understand your diagnosis), and gain weight.

Around this same time, one of my very best friends, Kellie (the clinical psychologist I mentioned a few chapters ago who supported me through my divorce), was diagnosed with stage 3 breast cancer. She was only thirty-six, and it was a horrific diagnosis for anyone, much less someone so young.

I was heartbroken for her, as she was still so young and vibrant and recently single. Our group of friends rallied around her, taking turns going to her chemo appointments, spending the night with her when she felt ill, holding her hair back when she was throwing up, and always doing what we could to make her laugh in light of the situation.

Guided by Grace

We even went with her to the salon when her hair started falling out and held hands with her while the stylist shaved off her beautiful, thick, silky, dark hair. I have to say, she was one of the most beautiful women I have ever known, and she was equally as stunning with no hair!

She chose to wear a wig most of the time, but on the occasions that she would take it off in our presence, I was always reminded of her bravery and was in awe of her stunning beauty and her big brown doe eyes that seemed to look through to one's soul. I will never forget how brave she was in facing her diagnosis. No doubt she was scared, but I was truly in awe of the courage she showed as she took on the most difficult challenge of her life.

Before she began chemo, Kellie had gone to a very reputable infertility treatment center to retrieve and freeze her viable eggs so that she could have a baby afterward if she chose to do so. She loved the female doctor who performed her procedure and recommended that I go to this renowned clinic in Beverly Hills.

It was extremely challenging to struggle with infertility while one of my best friends was fighting for her life with breast cancer. I tried not to talk about my challenges because I knew they paled in comparison to what she was dealing with.

It was quite ironic. Here we were, two women in our mid-thirties, supposedly at the most idyllic times of our lives, dealing with two very different challenges. Of course, my situation was not life or death, but often over the course of that two-year period, it felt like it. There were times when I felt like I was dying inside, wondering if I was being punished for wasting all of my viable reproductive years.

I knew deep down this was not the case, but I did quietly struggle with the thought that I had somehow created this situation for myself. I was finally in a happy, healthy relationship, and the thought that I wasn't going to be able to conceive a child started to consume me.

Jennifer Mentesana

As Kellie continued to focus on her chemo treatments and work in her psychology practice when she felt well enough, I went to more doctors to get to the bottom of my infertility. The doctor that Kellie referred me to ran some tests and found that my fallopian tubes were one hundred percent blocked on one side, and ninety-eight percent blocked on the other due to years of endometriosis (a condition where tissue from your uterine lining grows in other parts of your reproductive organs, often causing infertility).

No amount of Clomid or any hormone medication was going to fix that. I felt like a failure. One of the most natural, God-given gifts women have is to conceive, carry, and birth a child, and my body wasn't going to allow me to experience this gift. I was heartbroken. The head doctor who read the results of the test (he was the main fertility specialist in the practice) had the absolute worst bedside manner and gave me the news so abruptly and coldly that I started sobbing in his office with my husband sitting next to me, not sure what to do.

The doctor mentioned the words "in vitro fertilization," but I was so upset with the results and the way they were delivered that I didn't process anything he said. I don't remember if I even responded, but I do remember getting up and walking out of that office, thinking this journey was over. I explored options for solutions to endometriosis, which included surgery, but most studies found that the surgery recovery was painful and could not guarantee fertility.

Within a few months of that last diagnosis, I came home one day, completely stressed out from work, and told John I wasn't able to focus on anything. My nervous system was breaking down from the stress of the diagnosis and fear of never getting pregnant, as well as the constant pressure at work for our company to go public, and the sales department taking the brunt of the financial responsibility to keep the company afloat until we did.

After spending the next several weeks trying to accept the reality of my situation, I began searching for answers and a path forward. I found a fertility coach, someone who had gone through this journey as well, and our weekly meetings made a profound difference in my mindset.

I realized I had been approaching this process with the wrong lens. I had been relying solely on the practical, science-based methodology of infertility, yet what had made the biggest difference in my life in the past few years was my spiritual and mental growth. I began embracing the idea that I could treat my body like a temple, and prepare to *receive* a baby, focus on the medical science as well, but not put all my eggs in one basket—pun intended.

Finding my fertility coach and the years spent working with Mary Lee had opened me up to a whole new world. I became more open to the idea of challenging the beliefs that had plagued me for most of my life and exploring a new way of thinking and living.

I spent many hours journaling, going on long walks, and reading books that helped me expand my beliefs about life, energy, and how to manifest by embodying who and what you want in life. I started to understand more about the challenges that had plagued our family, including mental health, alcohol abuse, and our overall mindset.

While I was engrossed in researching about shifting my mindset, I stumbled upon a Facebook message about a meeting that was happening at a café in Hollywood about exploring the field of life coaching. Other than my fertility coach, I had never really heard of a life coach. I was curious, but more than that, I felt a subtle nudge of energy in my gut when I read the Facebook message, and I decided to trust it. (Yes, another **breadcrumb!**)

Remember, any time you feel a surge of energy in your body that is a result of something you've heard, felt, read, or seen, check in with where that feeling is coming from. Allow yourself to connect with the feeling and ask yourself, *Is this feeling excitement? Curiosity? Fear?*

Process what you are feeling and what that message could be telling you. For me, in that moment, that feeling was definitely curiosity and a little excitement. I would also say that there was a bit of fear of the unknown and of being uncomfortable exploring something so different, but as I had once tackled fear when I went skydiving to overcome my fear of heights, I knew I could manage whatever fear came up about this.

I went to the meeting that night, feeling a little uneasy, not sure what to expect, but excited about what could possibly be a new and interesting path for me. Little did I know that the decision to attend that meeting completely changed the trajectory of my life—again.

I figured that this was the ideal time to explore a new career path, something I could get excited about since it was aligned with the insights and beliefs that I was exploring. I took a chance, and I enrolled in a year-long life coach certification program while simultaneously going through my infertility journey. It seemed like the ideal way to connect mind, body, and spirit to my purpose. The tech boom was starting to slow down, as were the ad dollars coming in, and there were signs that our company, Spot Runner, would not be in business for much longer.

Within a few months of starting the certification program, I had an epiphany that was no doubt another **breadcrumb.** (Usually these come out of nowhere when you aren't even thinking about anything significant, but your mind and soul are open to receiving.)

Out of nowhere, I remembered I had a distant cousin who was a nationally renowned fertility doctor, and his office was only ten minutes from my house! It hadn't even occurred to me before this moment, and I really don't know why. I was so focused on finding a solution that my energy wasn't open to what the Universe was trying to tell me. I had gone back to my old ways of doing things, trying to force something to work in a particular way, when I had learned so many times that the outcome we are trying to create doesn't always come from the most obvious, logical path.

When you get out of your head and reconnect with your soul, your connection with the Universe and the divine, you are open to receiving the messages that guide you down the right path. I was so caught up in the outcome and the seemingly finality of it that I wasn't able to allow myself to connect with my higher self to see what *was* possible.

I was a little uncomfortable reaching out to my cousin since our families weren't close (the doctor was my dad's first cousin), and the fact that it would be awkward to think of having a family member giving me pelvic exams. But I was so ready to get on with the journey that I reached out to his office and left a message.

He called me back within a few hours and expressed his gratitude and relief that I had reached out. He promised me we would get to the bottom of what was going on and explore any and all options for me to conceive. Ironically, the acupuncturist I had been seeing for infertility was in the same building as the clinic.

It was all coming together. I felt momentum for the first time along this journey. Always trust momentum. When things are flowing and moving forward without resistance, and it feels right, trust that path, but make sure you are connected to your intuition and your inner voice. When it feels like you are pushing a boulder uphill, sometimes you need to pause, look around, and see if there is another less resistant way to the top.

Resistance is not always a sign that this is not the right path; in fact, resistance can be a sign that you are being tested for what's next. Never give up when you meet resistance; trust that there is a way forward, and look out for the path that unfolds before you.

So often in life, we push so hard to create the outcome we want that we lose sight of the valuable lessons and potential opportunities that can come from letting go and trusting the process. When you are holding on to something too tightly, it can't flow with the Universe. I was pushing so hard, trying to find answers to my infertility issues without connecting to my own higher power.

Allowing yourself to live in the flow of the Universe and connect with your higher power is the one true way to get through any difficult decision, challenge, or major obstacle. Sure, we must use reason to make decisions, but our intuition is more powerful than reason; it is infinite and has no boundaries. Reason is only based on what we have been taught, and there is only so far that it can take us. If reason isn't helping, we must let go of the need for control to figure it out and trust that God has a plan.

Please don't misunderstand; I am in no way saying give up, stop moving forward, or using logic. But what I am saying is slow down and stop pushing so hard for the answers, and allow your inner knowing to come through. If you can truly let go, get grounded, and trust that God will deliver, He will deliver exactly what is truly meant for you. It may not always look exactly like the path you hoped or the vision you have, but I can guarantee it will, in many ways, be more of a blessing than you can ever imagine.

After confirming that both of my fallopian tubes were completely blocked, my cousin confirmed that if I wanted to be pregnant, my only option was IVF. Exploring that journey was not only a major financial decision (one round of IVF can cost upwards of $30,000) but a spiritual process in which I had to connect deeply to my higher power to allow myself to believe that God wanted this for me.

I had to come to terms with knowing I was truly meant to carry a baby, and that it was okay for me to trust science. John and I grappled with this for quite a bit, but after praying on it and really taking the time to decide, we knew we would be blessed to be able to conceive in this way.

Our beliefs were that if God intends for us to have a child, it doesn't matter *how*. The *how* behind our decisions isn't always what matters most; what truly matters is whether those choices align with our core values, our shared beliefs as a couple, and our deeper sense of purpose. When our decisions come from a place of integrity and do no harm to others, how could they be outside of God's will? How could they not be part of our unique path or calling, like the desire to bring a child into the world?

Guided by Grace

Faith, religion, and culture shape beliefs in vastly different ways, and it's not our place to judge what is right or wrong for someone else. Our values and belief systems are deeply personal and woven into the fabric of who we are. As long as our beliefs do not bring harm to anyone, there is no such thing as a "wrong" core value.

When it comes to big questions about life, including God, and science, we're often met with a wide range of perspectives. For me, I believe we're blessed to have access to both. Science and faith are not mutually exclusive; in fact, I see science as one of the many gifts God has given us to understand the world more deeply.

This journey of acceptance was one of my first lessons in truly letting go of the outcome. I had to trust that IVF was going to work, and that ultimately I would be a mother somehow, someway, if that was what God intended for me.

Once I let go of the outcome, the process became so much more enjoyable, and I could finally relax. After two rounds of IVF, I was finally pregnant! I can honestly say, once we got the news, I was so profoundly grateful it didn't matter to me how it happened. The entire struggle had been worth it. The fact that I was finally going to accept a baby into the world at thirty-nine years old was all that mattered.

I was halfway through my coaching certification, and it felt like a whole new life was just beginning, not just for my unborn baby, but for both of us. It was a rebirth in more ways than one.

Jennifer Mentesana

Take this time to journal about an outcome you are so attached to that your grip feels unshakably tight, where you can almost feel the visceral pull of needing it to happen. For me, it was my desire to have a baby. I was so focused on the outcome and on figuring out how it was going to happen that I blocked the flow of positive energy and God's will.

Because I was pushing so hard, I cut myself off from receiving. I was operating in masculine energy, focused on logic, reason, action, and assertiveness, while the feminine energy of intuition, receptivity, and connection was missing.

How can you let go of the need to control the outcome, trust that God has a plan, and allow yourself to truly relax so you can receive? This takes time to fully embrace, but through journaling, a daily gratitude practice (which we will explore in a future chapter), and intentional self-care, you can gradually learn to trust.

Chapter 12
Full Circle

"To forgive is to set a prisoner free and discover that the prisoner was you."
–Lewis B. Smedes

Not long after I found out I was pregnant, my father called to tell me he had stage 4 stomach cancer, and he only had a few months left to live. He had been exploring treatment options with his doctor, and none of them were going to help him live; they would only make him more comfortable and prolong his life by a few months.

As you can imagine, this was such a strange place to be emotionally, as I was finally pregnant, but hearing the news about my dad left me feeling incredibly conflicted. My father had been dealing with health issues for my entire life, and he had survived colon cancer at forty, multiple heart attacks, kidney failure, several years of dialysis, and a kidney transplant. (His donor was a lifelong friend and colleague who happened to be a perfect tissue match.) I always believed my dad had nine lives, because grumpy, stressed, and unhealthy as he was, he always survived. But this time was different. He had never told me he was dying before.

I hadn't spent much time with my dad in my adult years after my parents' divorce. After the holidays in college that we would split between my mom's and my dad's, I only saw him maybe once per year, once I was out of school.

Throughout the years, before his kidney transplant, he made the effort to plan vacations when he was feeling up to it, and I did my best to enjoy the time with him. He was not easy to be with, and I found it challenging to find things to talk about. I would tell him about my career or some mundane details of my life, but we were never close, and never spoke about anything profound after he moved out of our home.

He and his wife, Barbara, moved to Tucson, Arizona, not long after his first kidney failure, when I was in my mid-twenties. He needed to get on a transplant list there since LA had a longer list than the years he had left to live. I visited him once a year on Thanksgiving or when I could, and I took John and Olivia to Arizona to meet him a year or two before John and I were married. Other than the couple of times that he came back to LA, my dad wasn't really present in our lives. I would call him once in a while to give him updates on our lives and to check in, but our conversations were strained and awkward.

I was conflicted about how to respond when he said he was dying. What do you say to your father (whom you never talk about anything real with) when he tells you he's dying, and there's nothing they can do?

I decided, because I had been so engrossed in my coach certification process and all the self-development I was working on, to open up to him and actually share my thoughts. I asked him questions that I would have never been comfortable asking him before. I asked him

Guided by Grace

what it felt like to hear the diagnosis from the doctor that he was dying. I asked him if he was scared.

His response surprised me. He opened up to me more than I could have ever expected. He shared that he had been grateful for his life, that he had a good life, had worked hard, and made many mistakes, but that he was okay with dying. He was in a place of acceptance, and I think in many ways somewhat relieved that he could finally let go of fighting.

My father was an atheist, which was mind-boggling to me, but it made sense after I asked him about that. I just didn't understand how he could not believe in something, and his answer was so sad to me. "I have seen no proof in my life that any God exists."

When I asked him how he could explain love, beauty, pure joy, or passion for something, his answer was, "I haven't seen or felt those things in so long, I have no reference." I felt sad for him. It wasn't simply that my dad was an atheist; it was his right to believe what he wanted. What struck me most was that he seemed to have no reference point for some of the deepest emotions and most beautiful gifts that make life truly meaningful.

My dad chose to live out the rest of his days quietly letting go. He traveled to San Diego, and I went down to visit him for a couple of days. It was a nice visit, and honestly, he seemed truly at peace. When Barbara called a month later to tell me he had been taken to hospice and that I should probably come out to see him soon, I knew it was the end. I called my brothers, and we all booked flights to Tucson. My youngest brother, Adam, couldn't get out on a flight right away, coming from Santa Cruz, CA, so Matt and I flew out from LAX to Tucson together.

The day we arrived, we rented a car and went straight to the hospice center. My dad was in relatively good spirits and was coherent and somewhat chatty. I had expected him to be far worse off, but he seemed almost happy just to see us, as if it were just another day.

After a few hours, we went back to the house to relax, get a bite, and wind down for the night. Matt stayed up most of the night, but being in my first trimester, I was exhausted, so I went straight to bed and got up early. I hardly slept that night. My mind was racing, and I was so worried about my early pregnancy and how the littlest thing might risk it that I couldn't rest.

I went back to the hospice center the next morning by myself, and my dad was in a completely different state. I realized how fortunate we had been to see him in good spirits the day before, and I decided to sit with him for several hours as the hospice nurses came in often to check on his status and make sure his medication kept him comfortable.

One of the nurses told me to hold his hand and provide constant touch, as it helps ease the process of his pain. This was a profound moment for me. Throughout my life, I rarely showed affection for my father, nor did he for me.

I felt uncomfortable at first, but I did it anyway. I held his hand, spoke to him kindly, told him he was a good father (even though he hadn't been in many ways, but he had done the best he could), and after a few minutes, I saw a tear slowly fall down his face.

All of the anger, stress, frustration, bitterness, and sadness over the years had come down to this moment. I was grateful to have it with him. I stayed with him until Matt showed up a few hours later. Adam was arriving on a flight in less than thirty minutes, and my only hope was that he would make it to say goodbye. I told my dad to hang on, that Adam was coming, and not to go anywhere.

Matt and I drove to the airport without saying a word. We both knew that he could be gone at any moment, but we needed to do our best to help Adam say goodbye. We prepared Adam for what to expect and raced back to the hospice center. I'm pretty sure I was speeding the entire way; thank goodness we didn't see any police on the drive from the airport.

Guided by Grace

When we walked back into the room, my father was clearly in his last moments of life, but he had waited for Adam. Adam told him he was there, and we all stood together around his bed, holding hands, saying goodbye. We prayed, cried, and Matt read a beautiful letter to him that he had stayed up all night to finish.

We told my father we loved him, and he took his last breath as I placed my hand on my belly where my baby was growing inside of me. It was such a wild experience, growing life inside of me, while witnessing my father's death. I prayed silently for my father's soul and that I had forgiven him for everything. In the end, we came together as a family to honor his life, and I felt peace.

I was fortunate to have those last few conversations with my father. I had come a long way from the young girl who needed her father's approval, attention, and love, and rarely ever received it. He couldn't show it, but I know he loved me in the best way he knew how. His way of showing love was being a provider and introducing his love of the outdoors to his kids. I was sorry that he was never going to meet his grandchildren or have them meet him. In the end, that wasn't part of the plan. He was who he was, and his entire life and who he became were a bigger gift and lesson than I could have ever imagined.

Forgiveness is necessary if you want to move forward in life. You cannot grow or become who you truly want and are meant to be if you are holding on to grudges or what-ifs. It's hard to forgive, especially when you have had horrific things done to you.

My father wasn't a bad person. I would even go out on a limb and say he was a good person who *tried very hard* but was extremely devoid of awareness, accountability, and purpose. He had not learned (until the very end) the valuable lessons of his life.

He was ill from the time he was twenty-one years old, but he always viewed his health issues as something that happened *to* him. He chose not to grow from the pain or turn it into purpose, which I believe is why he continued to get sick.

Jennifer Mentesana

He battled illness for almost forty-five years. Can you imagine never turning to faith, understanding, or growth but constantly battling, fighting, and pushing through the pain for forty-five years? It was a lesson I have taken with me since his death, and I am so grateful for it.

Don't waste a single day of your life being angry about what happened to you. Forgive, let go, trust, and, most of all, believe that regardless of your pain, suffering, or sadness, there is always a path forward if you choose to have faith.

> Is there someone in your life you need to forgive? What would happen if you chose, right now, to release the anger and resentment you have been carrying and allow your heart to forgive that person? How would it feel to let it all go, not just for them but for yourself?
>
> Take some time to journal about how it might feel to forgive and what could become possible once you release the weight. You do not even need to tell the person that you forgive them. Simply let go, offer forgiveness, and send love and prayers so that you can free your own heart.

Chapter 13
The Gift

*"Everything comes to us that belongs to us,
if we create the capacity to receive it."*
–Rabindranath Tagore

After my father died, I was knee-deep in my coach certification process. While I had that moment of peace and forgiveness, saying goodbye, I hadn't really processed a lot of what had happened. It had taken me so long to get pregnant, and I was so focused on the health of my baby and my pregnancy that I did not want to grieve. I wanted my body to be as calm and peaceful as possible to create this new little life inside of me.

Barbara, my stepmother, told us she was not planning any type of service for my father, and I completely understood. She had been through a lot caring for him all those years when he was so ill, and she was ready to move on.

My dad was cremated and had no real wishes on what to do with his ashes other than to have Barbara spread a portion of them over the

Jennifer Mentesana

seventeenth hole at their golf course in Tucson. My dad was not very sentimental, and being the oldest of my siblings, I felt compelled to, at least, explore the idea of having a small ceremony for some sort of closure, or out of respect for his memory. My brothers were indifferent to the idea, even when I suggested that we all go over to Catalina and spread his ashes where he loved to ride horses most of his adult life.

After a few conversations with my mom and my brothers, we decided to just let it go and not do anything to commemorate his life. After all, I was pregnant and going through certification and was leading this particular charge, and no one else wanted to take the reins. I regret that decision to this day. No matter what relationship you have with someone, when they are a part of your life, I believe it is important to commemorate their life, and their death in some capacity.

When you have something on your heart that you want to do, just do it. When my grandfather passed away by suicide at eighty-three years old (that's a story for another time), our immediate family took a boat out in the ocean off Long Beach, California, and spread his ashes.

I will have that memory forever, and the peace and process that came along with it were special. I don't have that with my father. My final memory with my father when he passed was extremely special, but I wish I had done something commemorative to honor his life.

I often think that's why I have so many mementos of him around my house—pictures of him riding his horse, and items from his home that I remember from my childhood. While I wasn't close to my dad most of the years of my life, that doesn't mean I didn't love him or that I don't miss him.

In fact, it's funny how when people die, our brains only want to remember the good things. I choose to remember the fun times with my dad. Riding on the trails of Alisal Ranch as a kid, or moments when he was in a good mood and was laughing and having fun.

Guided by Grace

Don't have regrets in life. They are a waste of energy and can keep you from your joy. Do the things that you are innately drawn to do. Don't wait until "someday" for something that is on your heart.

I went on that year with my certification, John was working, and life was pretty much cruising along. Kellie was in remission, and she called me one day to meet for lunch down by the beach. After we ate, we walked along the beach and talked. She was in such good spirits, and other than being in remission, I sensed that something else was going on.

She had met someone special, and I was so incredibly happy for her. I was surprised when she told me who it was, because he was a very famous rock star from the 1970s and 1980s. She told me that he had seen her in a scene from a documentary that she had been featured in about five women who were dealing with breast cancer. He was friends with the director, and the moment he saw her on screen, something profound told him that he needed to meet her. He didn't care that Kellie had breast cancer. He was enamored with her beauty, and I believe to this day, he was following a breadcrumb that he had received telling him that this woman was someone he needed to meet.

They spent almost five hours on the phone in their first conversation, and within a few meetings, they were falling in love. I was so profoundly happy for Kellie. She had been through hell and was finally finding the true love and respect she deserved from a man who adored her.

They went on trips to Hawaii, traveled the world together, and by the time I delivered my son in January 2010, they were living together. I felt at peace knowing I was finally bringing a child into the world, and Kellie was starting a whole new life in remission, with a man she loved. I was so grateful that while I was about to become a mom, she was finally happy and in love.

Motherhood came easily to me with Nicolas. He was a dream baby! There was no doubt in my mind that this boy was a true miracle and a gift from God. I had wanted him so badly and had prepared my mind, body, and soul for him to come into this world so that when he finally did, it was truly miraculous.

My friends have often said that he was such a calm and sweet baby because of my calm and peaceful energy during my pregnancy. I don't know if that's true, but it is entirely possible. The more at peace and calm you are, the more of that energy you bring to yourself and others. I honestly believe that God sent me the most precious soul who would bless our lives because I prayed for him every single day.

While I was embracing motherhood and coaching clients in my home office, which was a garage converted to an outdoor living space/office, I was so grateful to be home with my son, able to hear him through the monitor when he slept.

I had created the ideal life for myself and our family, allowing us to continue focusing on my passion for coaching and helping others while being home with my baby. It was truly a dream come true. John was thriving in his role as sales manager for a startup LA radio station, and things seemed to be finally coming together in alignment with all we had prayed for.

But here's the thing about life: there's no guarantee that phase will last forever. In fact, the only guarantee in life is that you *will* have adversity, challenges, hardships, and life-altering obstacles that come your way. It's how you choose to deal with those challenges that ends up being your reality. You can choose to wallow in the challenges and ask yourself why things are happening to you, or you can choose to look at all of the good that is around you and relish that. Either way, it's up to you how you choose to look at your life, in the good times, as well as the difficult.

About a year after Nicolas was born, my husband walked in the door early from work. I wasn't expecting him home, and I immediately knew something was wrong. He had been let go from his job, a role he had poured his heart into for almost three years.

Guided by Grace

He was crushed. But soon after the disappointment wore off, he came to me one evening when I was putting Nicolas down and said, "I think it's time to go after my dream of opening a restaurant." He had told me when we first met that "one day, when he didn't need the money," he wanted to open a restaurant. His upbringing was rooted in food, but not just eating; every conversation, get-together, and activity was rooted in Italian culture and cooking.

When he was young, his grandmother, from Naples, Italy, lived with his family, and she taught him and his brother Frank how to make pizza dough from scratch. He wanted to open a Neapolitan pizzeria (the original pizza from Naples) as this type of pizza was just being introduced on the West Coast. There were several Neapolitan pizzerias in New York and elsewhere on the East Coast, but we would be one of the first authentic Neapolitan pizzerias in Los Angeles.

I was excited about his entrepreneurial spirit and his desire to go after his dreams. Of course, I was on board but knew that we were going to have to make some changes if I was going to help him launch his dream restaurant. I continued to coach clients and raise Nicolas while we were still in the early stages of planning.

Fortunately, John's brother Frank helped us write the business plan, as he had owned and operated a restaurant in New York City for many years and had been in the food business in some capacity all his adult life. They came up with recipes for salads and starters, and some unique pairings for signature pizzas.

The three of us did all the research, scouted locations, hosted tastings for investors, and even took a trip up to Northern California to train with a professional *pizzaiolo* (Italian for pizza maker) who had trained in Italy. It took almost two years before we settled on a location in Redondo Beach, California.

Meanwhile, I became pregnant (miraculously without IVF) with our second son, Andrew, and our life was beginning to pick up speed. I thrived in the excitement of growth and opportunity and embraced every moment of entrepreneurship. We had finally begun construction on our location when I got a call from Kellie, who wanted me to come up to North Hollywood to see her. She had come back from New York, and cancer had come back with a vengeance.

When I arrived at her home in the Hollywood Hills, she was visibly weak and had clearly been suffering for several months. The last time I had spoken to her, she had been in New York as part of a new experimental cancer treatment trial that was working so well that she was feeling better than ever. She had been exercising again, practicing yoga, and living a quintessential life in New York with her boyfriend. It had taken her almost three months to contact me and let me know that the treatment had failed and had been only a temporary glimpse of life cancer-free.

We sat outside looking over the landscape of the San Fernando Valley. Her voice was almost monotone, but peaceful, and she talked about how beautiful everything was and how, in that moment, time seemed to stand still. I could clearly see how something was very different in her. I couldn't pinpoint it, but I was in awe of her calm and peaceful demeanor when she was clearly in pain.

She had lost most of her hair again and had been through several rounds of radiation as the cancer had spread to her brain. As the afternoon became dusk, we went inside to relax on the couch, and I poured us each a cup of tea.

Although Kellie was feeling weak and needed me to assist her to the couch, she insisted that I stay longer. As we sat on the giant sectional in the middle of this massive living room, looking out through the floor-to-ceiling windows to the lights of the valley below, we talked for at least another hour.

She asked me about the progress of the restaurant and how motherhood was. I felt ashamed speaking about my joy when she was clearly suffering, but she insisted that I share it all. I finally got the courage to

Guided by Grace

ask her how she was feeling about her treatment and what her plan was. She told me she was done fighting. It had been almost five years since her first diagnosis. She wasn't angry, but calm, as if this sense of peace and knowing had come over her. She told me that she wasn't afraid to die, and that she was coming to terms with it.

It was such an incredibly difficult conversation because I wanted to scream at her and tell her not to give up! But she wanted the space to talk about it. I could tell that she wasn't able to share how she was really feeling with her boyfriend and her mom because they were pushing her so hard to fight.

I wanted to be there for her to express herself any way she wanted. She was only forty years old and should have had her whole life ahead of her! She had finally found the love of her life, who treated her the way she deserved to be treated, and it just didn't seem right that she wasn't going to be able to live out her dreams.

All her life, she had helped people. She had helped me get through my divorce from Tom and helped countless others dealing with horrific challenges. Her gift was that she wanted to help young girls gain the confidence and faith that they could be anything they wanted to be and not be limited by their circumstances.

Kellie had had a difficult childhood and had overcome so much and managed to get herself through grad school at UCLA while waiting tables, and received her doctorate in psychology. Here she was, this incredible, smart, beautiful, and selfless woman who had lived to help others, now dying before she could ever get married, have a child, and see them grow up.

It was heartbreaking, and I wanted to scream and beg her to fight. I told her I wasn't giving up and that I would pray for her every day. And then, together we prayed, holding hands and crying, just as her boyfriend walked through the door.

They both walked me to the front door, with him holding onto her, as she was almost too weak to stand by that point. They smiled, arm in arm, as we said goodbye, and I cried and prayed all the way home that she would not give up.

A month later, I received a call on an early December morning that she had passed away just a few hours before. I dropped to the floor. I just couldn't believe it. Even though I considered the fact that she wouldn't make it, it didn't occur to me that she would be gone so quickly, and that would be the last time I would ever see my beautiful friend. I now know that she had asked me to come see her so she could say goodbye. It was the greatest gift she could have ever given me.

Life isn't a guarantee. Nothing in this life is ever one hundred percent. The only thing you can truly rely on is your faith and trust that God has a plan for all of us. It may not work out the way we think or hope, but we must do the best we can with what God gives us.

It's up to us to create the life that we want and to listen to the nudges, the breadcrumbs from the Universe, to go down the path that we were born to live so that we can truly live in our purpose, no matter how long we have on this earth. It could be a lifetime, forty years, or ten; we just never know.

The gift is the lesson that we have in this lifetime to become the version of ourselves that we were born to be. I know that Kellie lived that to the fullest, and that she was innately and divinely brought into my life to teach me that lesson, as well as so many others. She lived her life unapologetically, in her purpose, and while she was treated horribly by others (especially men), she was always there for everyone. She finally found real love, even if only for a short time, and in the end, I know she was at peace.

Do you know what your true purpose in this lifetime is? Have you ever even thought about it? Maybe you feel that your purpose is to be a mom, or you have a calling to care for others as a nurse or doctor. Maybe, like Kellie, you want to help people get through challenging times and give back in some way.

Guided by Grace

At that point in my life, with two young boys, a husband, and a new business, my purpose was completely rooted in caring for my family. Everything about my innate core purpose had been pushed to the side since my goal, once I met and married John, had been all about having a family.

> Take a moment to journal about what you believe your true purpose is in this lifetime. Do you know it immediately, or do you need time to think about it? Do you even believe you have a true purpose, and have you ever considered that you have the right to pursue it?
>
> I hope you do, because you have spent a lot of time reading this book, and I want you to know that you were put on this earth for a reason. Take some time to really think about it and feel it. Sit quietly for as long as you can, and let go of the thoughts in your head about what you need to do right now.
>
> Trust that this moment is for you to connect with your higher power and your intuition. Just listen. What is your gut telling you about what you are meant to do in this lifetime? What gifts and talents do you know are uniquely yours? How does it feel when you are using them? Do you feel alive, happy, and fulfilled? How do those talents connect to what you do every day?
>
> Keep journaling and see what comes up before you move on to the next chapter. And if you find yourself struggling, that is okay. The point is simply to begin connecting with your higher power and trusting the inner knowing that will guide your path.

Chapter 14
The Only Way Around Is Through

"Being challenged in life is inevitable; being defeated is optional."
–Roger Crawford

It took some time to process that Kellie was really gone. When you lose someone, it's always difficult, especially if it's a family member. But when you lose someone so young, before their time, or so you believe, it takes time to come to terms with the *why*. There are a lot of questions like, "Why her and not me?" and "Why now, when she finally found someone who truly loved her?" These are the answers that only come in God's time, but when they do come, it all makes sense.

Kellie's service was spectacular. It was a true celebration of life in every sense of the word. At one point during one of the readings, I actually felt her sitting next to me. Her presence was everywhere, and we all felt it!

Then, during a moment of silence, one of her boyfriend's most popular songs was played, and it was so apropos to her, this moment, and the life she lived and left behind. We all got up and started dancing, crying, and singing together in the middle of that beautiful church in North Hollywood. It was remarkable, and I know she was relishing everyone she loved singing, dancing, and celebrating her life together!

I believe that Kellie, like many who die so young, died because her time on this earth was complete. All of the lessons and purpose that she was meant to live for had been executed. She spent her adult life helping others, caring for others, and living out her gifts and talents to truly see others for who they are. I felt that she left behind a legacy that I wanted to live up to.

She overcame countless obstacles, including a very difficult childhood, putting herself through college and grad school, and going from broke to success all on her own. It was now time for her to move on, and that was it.

My best friend, Jen, said something so beautiful after Kellie died. Kellie passed away in the early morning hours of December 14th, just a few hours before the Sandy Hook Elementary shooting that killed six adults and twenty children.

The day we were planning Kellie's service, Jen said, "I believe God took Kellie that morning so that she could be there to greet all of those babies in Heaven!" She hadn't been able to have her own children, but she could be there for these precious souls when they arrived. No matter what you believe, it's always helpful to find the good and be comforted by the idea that God has a bigger plan. Because He always does. And that is true in life and in death.

That period further solidified my mission to be rooted in meaning. Kellie and I often spoke about working together to help young women find their power and confidence. We were both young women who had been deprived of that for too long, and we wanted to help young girls and young women who were just like us.

We had talked about starting a program for teenage girls to guide them through those formative years when they are trying to figure out who

Guided by Grace

they are, and when they can often make the decisions that take them off course.

With Kellie gone and having completed my coaching certification, I became further rooted in my purpose. I wanted to give back and not just constantly be on the hamster wheel of survival. So many years of my life up to this point were spent worrying about things, mostly finances and security. I was tired of survival, and I was ready to make an impact in some way. I didn't know what that meant, or what it looked like, but between raising my two young boys and launching our restaurant, I didn't have much time to process those feelings, and again, they were put on the back burner.

It took another year before construction on our restaurant was complete, and we were finally ready to open our doors. With every hiccup you can think of, from permits to construction timelines and mishaps, city and county inspections, and everything in between, it was beyond delayed. We signed our lease for the space on August 1, 2013, and didn't open our doors until July 11, 2014.

However, the mid-summer timing was perfect, as we were opening in a beach town. We had a line out the door every night our first month! It was truly an incredible feeling to spend so much time and energy on something and see it come to fruition. All of the planning, hard work, and roadblocks were finally behind us, and we could start connecting to our community through food and hospitality.

That first year, we provided a lot of education in the community about the quality and authenticity of our food and why this type of pizza is unique. It was fun to introduce a new product, and I thrived in connecting with our patrons and creating partnerships.

I began doing a lot of community outreach, partnering with schools, fundraisers, and anything that made sense for us to collaborate on. Our restaurant's name, Locale90, is all about being local (hence the name "locale," which in Italian means "local"). The "90" was initially meant to highlight the length of time it takes for the pizza to bake in a wood-fired oven—ninety seconds—but also the first two numbers represent zip codes in Southern California. Our plan was to open multiple locations, all in Southern California, and after two years of being open, we were ready to expand. Or so we thought.

We scouted locations for several months all over LA, and when we found our second location just a few miles up the road in Hermosa Beach, we were beyond ecstatic. We wanted something further north, closer to the bustling town of Manhattan Beach, but without the high rent. (So much for that thought, considering our rent in Hermosa was almost double that of our first location.)

The space was originally a sushi restaurant and then, more recently, a high-end burger joint. We gutted the inside, picked out a gorgeous new black-tiled pizza oven, zinc countertops, and sanded down the wood-planked twenty-foot ceilings. We opened the front of the restaurant with garage door–style patio doors so that guests could dine while looking out at the beach just a block away.

It was truly a gorgeous remodel. John and I were so proud of how it turned out, and with all the success we had in our first location, we knew it was going to be a huge hit for this little beach town community.

We had a fabulous private opening week, connecting with friends and community members from all over to let them experience the new location, and we opened our doors officially in early December 2016.

We did not plan for the monsoonal rains that would follow in the winter of 2017. I mean it rained in Southern California for three months straight, and we quickly realized we were going to need to sell a lot of pizzas once spring came around to keep this business afloat until we made it to the busy summer months.

From day one, that location was a challenge, and we were barely scraping by. We decided to focus a lot of time, energy, and money not only on marketing and community outreach, but also on catering and events. We had developed a busy and successful catering arm with a mobile wood-fired oven.

Guided by Grace

We became known all over the South Bay for making fresh pizzas on-site at homes or event venues. To keep Hermosa afloat until we could get some momentum, we decided to put together a specific catering and events department. The Hermosa location was large enough to host events of up to eighty-five people, and we began looking for a professional catering manager who had experience with execution as well as sales.

We hired a young woman who had an extensive résumé in catering and food management, and we were off and running. By now, we had over fifty staff members working for us, and with managing two restaurants (open seven days a week) and raising two young boys, it was a lot of juggling.

We were starting to feel spread really thin and were overwhelmed. I spent my mornings getting the boys off to school, doing my rounds at each restaurant, and then racing back to pick the kids up from school and take them to their afternoon sports and activities. I never really felt grounded in one place, being pulled in so many different directions, but I knew if we could just hang in there for another year or so, it would all pay off.

Fortunately, after about a year, we started to see a little progress in the Hermosa Beach restaurant (after multiple managers came and went, as well as countless servers and kitchen staff). One thing that you don't realize when you get into the restaurant business is that, while the work is extremely rewarding, the staffing is beyond challenging.

Not everyone who works for you is going to have as much passion for your business as you do, not even close. That is the case with any type of business, but in the restaurant business, most of your employees are only there to collect a paycheck. They are all about themselves for the most part (although there are a rare few you find who you must hang on to for dear life!), and it's a constant revolving door.

Just when we would train and invest in a new employee and get them up to speed, they would turn around and quit for whatever reason.

Jennifer Mentesana

There's very little loyalty, and it was up to us to make the best possible working environment so that our employees wanted to stay as long as possible.

It's also a challenge to find good servers who genuinely want to provide good service. The ones who do are amazing and can make all the difference in the guest experience, but the ones who are only there to punch the clock can be devastating for business, not only with the guests but with morality and a team environment.

John and I have always prioritized creating a team-oriented culture in our restaurants, built on mutual respect, professionalism, and a shared commitment to giving our guests the best possible experience, no matter what's going on behind the scenes.

Most of the time, that culture thrives. But every so often, we've encountered team members who aren't aligned with those values, whether due to a poor attitude or deeper personal struggles, like substance abuse.

Those moments are the hardest. Over the years, we've had employees show up to work under the influence of drugs or alcohol. It's heartbreaking to witness, especially knowing addiction is a disease. We've cared so much that at one point, we even offered to pay for rehab for someone. But we've also learned that no matter how much we want to help, people have to be ready and willing to help themselves.

As much as we lead with compassion, we've also had to set clear boundaries. Second and third chances rarely lead to a change in these situations. We've learned that sometimes the most loving thing we can do for our team, our business, and even the individual, is to let go and trust that their healing journey has to be their own.

Everything you do in life offers a chance to learn. There is a lesson in everything, and you can choose to learn from it or keep making the same mistakes over and over again. In the case of the Hermosa restaurant location, we had yet to experience the lesson, but the reality would soon take hold.

Guided by Grace

Thank goodness the catering and events business had taken off, and we were grateful for the income to keep us afloat. In the fall of 2019, we were almost breaking even, and we were hopeful that the coming year would be a year of growth and expansion.

More than half of our income from the business in Hermosa Beach was coming from events, and fortunately, with the 2019 holiday season, we had two to three events booked each week. When the pandemic hit in early 2020, we knew there was no way we could stay afloat without being able to host indoor events or even indoor dining.

We had only been open three years, but it was three full years of struggle with not much reward. We had seven more years still left on our ten-year lease, and we had poured $500,000 of our own money (which we had been saving to buy a house) into that restaurant to get it remodeled and up and running. We had seen zero profit and more heartache and struggle than we thought possible.

We were fortunate to negotiate with our landlord, and we got out of our lease in early April 2020, thank goodness. We still had to continue paying off what we owed, but at least we were not on the hook for the remainder of the lease. That stung. We took a big hit, and it was the first real, seemingly insurmountable challenge we encountered in our business. There were others, but nothing that hit quite like the failure of our Hermosa Beach location.

John took it extremely hard as he had never really experienced a challenge of this magnitude. He used to say to me, "Everything just comes easily to me." I used to envy that confidence, but then I realized that wasn't necessarily a good thing. If everything comes easily to you in life, then you don't learn how to overcome when things get hard.

John had been successful in sales since graduating from college and had never really seen any personal failure. He thrived in his career until the day he was let go from his radio management role. He was able to shift that challenge quickly because he focused on his passion for food, and we were in it together.

Jennifer Mentesana

I had been muscling through for most of my adult life, so while this was devastating, especially financially, the idea of failure didn't hit me as hard as it did my husband. Failures are there so we can learn. If you haven't failed at anything, then you aren't trying, growing, or becoming who you are designed to be. If you don't take risks and learn the lessons, you will never actualize your full potential.

The other effects of the pandemic were almost inconceivable to me. At first, of course, I was concerned, like everyone else, but as the weeks and months went on, it started to occur to me that something was very wrong with this scenario.

I don't know how to explain it, but what was happening almost felt contrived and not natural. It was going against the natural law of the Universe and humanity. Human beings are social creatures who need connection for survival. It didn't make sense to me that people were forced to stay indoors and needed permission from others to create connection.

It didn't take long for me to share my feelings with some close friends, some of whom agreed, while others didn't, which was what we were all experiencing at that time. If there's one thing I've learned, especially during uncertain times like the pandemic, it's to *always* trust your intuition. That inner voice, your internal compass, is connected to your heart, soul, and gut. It knows the way, even when the world feels chaotic. During the pandemic, I relied on that compass more than ever. I trusted my inner knowing, my faith in God, and the values that anchor our family.

While fear swept through our communities, and many followed mandates they didn't fully understand, I chose a different path, not from rebellion, but from discernment. I understood why others were afraid, and I held compassion for that.

But for me, I couldn't subscribe to decisions that didn't align with my truth or my family's well-being. We continued to live in a way that felt grounded and intentional, riding bikes to the sandwich shop, spending

Guided by Grace

time outdoors, going to the beach, horseback riding, and letting our kids play with their friends. That's what felt right for us.

Yes, there were stares. Even harsh words from strangers yelling at us to wear masks while biking outdoors. But I knew in my heart that our choices were rooted in love and faith, not defiance. And I trusted that the people who truly knew us would understand and respect our values.

That season was eye-opening. It taught me the power of standing firm in my truth, even when it's unpopular. It reminded me that we don't have to justify our lives to others. We can take in advice, hear concerns, and still choose what's best for us.

Your life is *yours*. No one else is living it for you. So don't let anyone else dictate how you live it. Surround yourself with people who honor your values and who support you for who you truly are, regardless of their own beliefs. If they don't, that's okay. Sometimes, it's just a sign to find a new circle that aligns with your growth and beliefs. That doesn't mean you should disrespect their beliefs—they have the right to them as well. Just trust that you know deep down what is right for you and your family.

One of the greatest gifts the pandemic gave me was clarity. Clarity about what matters most, who I want to be, and how I want to lead my family. And through it all, I witnessed the beauty of our Redondo Beach business community showing up for one another with heart and resilience. That kind of connection and courage is something I'll always be grateful for.

We still had our original location in Redondo Beach, and while indoor dining had been shut down, we could still offer takeout. Like millions of other businesses across the country, we did what we could to survive the pandemic, and we quickly realized a need for fresh, quality home-baked meals that were also fun to make.

Parents and families were desperate for new ideas to cook since take-out was not only expensive, but no one wanted to eat take-out more than a couple of times per week. We created our Neapolitan pizza kits for families to pick up and take home and bake. It was a fun and delicious activity for the whole family, and even young kids could get in on the action, stretching the dough and topping their own pizzas.

Within a few months, we were delivering pizza kits all over the South Bay and had even partnered with a local nonprofit to provide pizza kits to families in need. It was such a rewarding experience to witness these families sharing videos of themselves creating memories with our food.

When you are going through adversity, always remember, what feels like a setback is often a setup for something greater. That's exactly what happened when we closed our doors in Hermosa Beach. Without the pandemic, we would never have created the idea for take-and-bake pizza kits, which are now a staple in our restaurant and also birthed other creative ideas.

Instead of opening several restaurant locations, we started to see the momentum in food manufacturing and product launches. This was born out of necessity during the pandemic and out of our true authenticity as a business and a brand. We had opened the Hermosa Beach location primarily to check the boxes of the goal we were chasing. We hadn't really decided on our *why* behind opening that second location or even the one beyond that.

We were so focused on our plan for execution that we had lost track of our *why* in the first place. John's original purpose was to share his passion for really good quality food with our community and educate our patrons on the authenticity of Neapolitan pizza.

Beyond that, there was no real purpose. We based our goals and our decision to open multiple locations in ten years on the expectations of investors and a sound business model. There was no real passion behind opening multiple locations, only the desire to grow and scale for financial reasons.

When we saw the momentum with the pizza kits and ultimately our par-baked, frozen Neapolitan pizzas, we realized that this was the window the Universe was opening. Now all we had to do was trust it and move forward.

Often, when we go through challenges, we are so knee-deep that we can't see the lesson or the opportunity in the challenge. We ask ourselves, *Why is this happening? What did I do wrong?* Or my favorite, *Maybe I'm just not meant to be successful* (that one had creeped into my subconscious more often than I care to admit).

Instead of viewing the challenge as a growth period that is necessary to get to the next level of life and opportunity, we often view it as a roadblock to our dreams. But maybe, just maybe, it's actually the thing we need to experience and overcome so that we can get to the next level of growth and potential.

Again, if you never have challenges, how will you learn to be successful? As I said in the previous chapter, the only guarantee in life is that you will have challenges that you need to overcome, and truly, the only way around them is through them.

> Are you currently facing a challenge in your life that you could also see as an opportunity for growth? Every challenge carries the potential for learning and transformation. How can you reframe what you are going through right now as preparation for the next great period of growth in your life?
>
> Take some time to journal about a challenge you are facing and what it might mean for you to overcome it. Allow it to become an opportunity for success and growth. More importantly, once you identify it, give yourself permission to fully feel the emotions that come with the challenge. Go through it, rather than dismissing it or trying to go around it. If you miss the lesson, you will likely repeat it. The only way forward is through.

Chapter 15
When the Universe Speaks, Jump!

"The universe is always conspiring to help us, if we only trust its wisdom."
−Ralph Waldo Emerson

I poured myself into the business for the next two years, trusting the momentum of the Universe and what I believed to be our next path forward, while John decided to go back to corporate America to help recover some of the financial loss we experienced from closing our Hermosa Beach location.

My boys were back in school full-time after they had been on Zoom for almost two years (believe me, I will someday write about the impact of this in a future book), and I was able to spend more time focusing on reconnecting with our community and developing our products.

I spent countless hours researching online retail opportunities, connecting with grocery stores, local retail businesses, and options for shipping products across the country. We had a lot of success early on, and then a lot of stops and starts. It was a rollercoaster of trial and error, and although I believed in the product, that aching feeling that something was missing came back with a vengeance.

As I have said countless times, when you feel something in the pit of your stomach, and you choose to ignore it, it gets louder and louder until you can't ignore it anymore. Sometimes you can mask it, or numb the feeling through addictions such as alcohol, shopping, gambling, or whatever you choose, but eventually you will have to face it one way or another.

Most of us did our share of overindulging during the pandemic. I certainly was one of the typical working moms who were exhausted from working and homeschooling my kids (even though they had classes on Zoom, we were still technically homeschooling), and cooking and cleaning all the time because everyone was *always* home.

It was a never-ending hamster wheel or Groundhog Day, whichever metaphor you prefer. The only saving grace I found was my morning walks once the kids were set up on Zoom. I looked forward to my forty-five minutes of quiet or a podcast to shift my mindset. It was a natural desire to want a glass of wine or two, or even three, every night and binge-watch our favorite shows just to escape.

But once the pandemic passed and life got somewhat back to normal, I realized just how much I had been drinking. It disturbed me, and I realized how much I had been numbing my feelings about everything that had happened over those years, our failed restaurant, parenting, the world, politics, our finances, the pandemic, and just about any other thing in life that had been going on at that time.

I did my best during the day to focus on the positive, to keep moving forward, and to find joy in the little things, but everything just felt heavy and exhausting. By the time dinner was over and the dishes were taken care of, all I wanted to do was check out. It was as if the hangover of the pandemic had set in, and I couldn't escape it, so the only thing to do was numb it away.

Guided by Grace

I've never been one to allow anything to have control over me, and I certainly didn't like the idea of becoming beholden to alcohol to get through. I had always told myself I was a social drinker, but it had become much more than that during the pandemic and was becoming part of my daily routine. I found myself irritable all the time and impatient with my kids. I wasn't really finding joy in anything, and I was only looking forward to the quiet moments when I could be alone or veg out and numb myself. All of this started coming to a head when I had a panic attack in the middle of the night. And when I woke up that morning, I knew it was time to make some changes.

First off, I needed to take a good look at my life and recognize all that I was grateful for. Here I was, fifty-two years old, with a beautiful family, a recovering business, and a wonderful group of friends. Life really wasn't that bad. Yes, we were struggling financially, but we were starting to get back on our feet again, so what was the issue? Why was I feeling so hopeless? I knew that drinking every night wasn't helping, and so that was the first thing I addressed. I changed my habits immediately.

Instead of plopping down on the couch with a glass of wine, a seltzer, or a vodka soda, I went into the bedroom and read a book. I lit a candle and gave myself space to be quiet and go inward. I began praying every morning before getting out of bed, then journaling afterward to let the connection with God flow onto the page.

After prayer and journaling, I added a daily gratitude practice, spending at least ten minutes focusing on five things I was grateful for each day. At first, they were small, like being thankful that my kids were healthy and safe. Over time, my gratitude grew, and I started to see light through the darkness.

Beginning each morning with the feeling of gratitude set the tone for my day. When I started that way, the energy usually carried through, shaping how the rest of the day unfolded.

This gave me the insight I needed to remember the things about my life that truly light me up and give me joy. Of course, my two boys, Olivia, and John, are part of it, but what did I truly love about myself? That was a hard one to answer for a while. I needed to remember who I was, before being a mom, a wife, and a business owner, and get back to what truly gives me joy.

For a long time, I lost sight of that. I started living for everyone else but myself. I was so focused on the success of our business, my husband, my boys, Olivia, my friends, and our community. I was a serial volunteer, spending hours on causes and the needs of others.

While all of this was noble and rewarding, it drained me of the precious time I needed to reconnect to my purpose and my soul. I had given so much and had left nothing for myself in return. I would tell myself that my time with my girlfriends going out and drinking together at dinner or brunch was time for me. And as much as I love doing that and connecting with some of my favorite people, it wasn't fueling my soul.

In fact, I found that it took away from my joy because it wasn't rooted in the type of connection I needed at that time. I was craving a transformative connection after the pandemic and something more than just a social hour. I started to research ways that I could create more connection for myself and other women who might be feeling the way I was. There had to be countless women in my community alone who could relate.

I went on a mission to find that community. As I rehashed the vision from the night of my panic attack, I researched ways that I could use my passion for public speaking and connecting, and another **breadcrumb** dropped in my lap. It occurred to me that I could create a podcast for women to tell their stories of motherhood, entrepreneurship, and the resilience that had gotten them through challenging times, and these stories could help other women!

The idea felt so amazing as I journaled about it. I immediately began researching podcasts to listen to different styles, niches, and interview formats. Remember what I said about paying attention when you start to feel excited, like you are about to jump out of your chair? Yes! That's a **breadcrumb** that you need to follow!

Over the next few months, I must have listened to dozens of different podcasts, but I kept coming back to this one called *True Grit and Grace* with Amberly Lago. I loved her authenticity and the genuine way she connected with her guests. I also loved her southern drawl, which reminded me of my college girlfriends from Texas.

The more I listened to Amberly's show, the more I felt drawn to her story of resilience and her ability to connect with people. Finally, I got the courage to reach out to her through her website, and not even a few days later, she responded! I couldn't believe it.

At this point, she was a world-renowned best-selling author, highly coveted motivational speaker, podcast host, and entrepreneur, and I didn't expect to receive a response that quickly, much less directly from her. I thought I would get a generic email from one of her assistants vetting me out first. But that's just how Amberly rolls. She's as authentic in person as she is on her show, and I immediately connected with her when we decided to meet via Zoom. I told her about my desire to start a podcast, speak publicly about entrepreneurship, and share my story. What is so incredible about Amberly is how, in just one meeting over Zoom, she was able to see in me what I couldn't quite yet see in myself. She recognized my gifts and talents as a communicator and connector and reminded me of that immediately.

Always surround yourself with people who truly *see* you—those who recognize your strengths, your gifts, your unique essence, and believe in your potential even when you're still finding your way. If you're fortunate, that belief starts with your parents. But even if it doesn't, your journey isn't lost. You must believe in yourself enough to stay the course, do the inner work, and trust that the right mentor, partner, or soul-aligned supporter will eventually reflect the light you carry inside.

Your true purpose often reveals itself not in grand, obvious moments, but in the small, sacred ones. The moments that feel effortless and joyful, where time stands still, is often where you are truly in the flow. These are the precious **breadcrumbs**. They show up when you're living in alignment with who you *already* are.

While people around you may not always say it out loud, if you asked someone who truly loves you to name one of your greatest gifts, they would answer without hesitation. That's your clue. That's your compass. Spend as much time as you can in that space, ideally through your work, and certainly in your daily life, using your natural gifts to impact the world around you.

This is where purpose lives. This is where joy begins.

So, follow the breadcrumbs.

If there's one message I hope this book has made clear, it's this: The breadcrumbs from God and the Universe are never random. They are your divine compass, nudging you gently but persistently toward the life you were always meant to live.

You can choose to ignore them and to quiet the whispers, but they will keep showing up until you listen. And when you do, your path will unfold with clarity, beauty, and purpose.

Now, as you turn the final page, I invite you to begin your *next* chapter, not just in this book, but in your life.

Take the first step.

Listen for the whisper.

Follow the nudge.

Say yes to the **breadcrumb** right in front of you.

Your purpose is not ahead of you; it's already *within* you, waiting to be remembered, embraced, and shared with the world.

Your next chapter starts now.

References

From page xxi

Brian Weiss, Author
Many Lives, Many Masters – 1988
Only Love Is Real – 1996

Andy Tomlinson & Reena Kumarasingham, Authors
Between Lives – 2025

Andy Tomlinson, Author
Exploring the Eternal Soul – 2012

Dr. Michael Newton, Author
Journey of Souls – 1994
Wisdom of Souls – 2019

THANK YOU FOR READING MY BOOK!

DOWNLOAD YOUR FREE GIFTS
Just to say thanks for buying and reading my book, I would like to give you a free bonus gift, no strings attached!

Scan the QR Code:

I appreciate your interest in my book and value your feedback, as it helps me improve future versions. I would appreciate it if you could leave your invaluable review on Amazon.com with your feedback.
Thank you!

www.ingramcontent.com/pod-product-compliance
Lightning Source LLC
Chambersburg PA
CBHW030248010526
44107CB00031B/1357/J